THE
DAMASCUS TEXTS

Companion to the Qumran Scrolls, 1

THE
DAMASCUS
TEXTS

Charlotte Hempel

 Sheffield
Academic Press

To Dick with love

Copyright © 2000 Sheffield Academic Press

Published by Sheffield Academic Press Ltd
Mansion House
19 Kingfield Road
Sheffield S11 9AS
England
http://www.shef-ac-press.co.uk

Printed on acid-free paper in Great Britain
by The Cromwell Press
Trowbridge, Wiltshire

British Library Cataloguing in Publication Data

A catalogue record for this book is available
from the British Library

ISBN 1-84127-055-5

Contents

Part II
4Q265 MISCELLANEOUS RULES (*olim* SEREKH DAMASCUS)

Preface

This book was written while I was Sutasoma Research Fellow at Lucy Cavendish College, Cambridge. The community at Lucy provided me with a very warm and supportive environment for writing for which I am very grateful. I further much appreciated and benefited from the scholarly exchanges with friends and colleagues in the Faculties of Divinity and Oriental Studies at Cambridge, both in and outside of formal seminars. I am grateful in particular to Professor Stefan Reif for kindly making available to me his entry on the Cairo Genizah for the *Encyclopedia of the Dead Sea Scrolls* prior to its publication. I also gained much from many conversations either in person or via the internet with friends and colleagues further afield. I further wish to thank the editor of the series, Professor Philip Davies, for asking me to write this volume and for his abundant patience in waiting for the arrival of the manuscript on his desk. Finally, thanks to my husband Dick who has yet again excelled at offering boundless amounts of encouragement, support, and fun while I worked on this book.

ABBREVIATIONS

ANYAS	*Annals of the New York Academy of Sciences*
BA	*Biblical Archaeologist*
BJS	Brown Judaic Studies
BZAW	Beihefte zur *ZAW*
CBQ	*Catholic Biblical Quarterly*
CRINT	Compendia rerum iudaicarum ad Novum Testamentum
DJD	Discoveries in the Judaean Desert
HeyJ	*Heythrop Journal*
HNTSP	*Harvard New Testament Seminar Papers*
HTR	*Harvard Theological Review*
JANES	*The Journal of the Ancient Near Eastern Society*
JBL	*Journal of Biblical Literature*
JJS	*Journal of Jewish Studies*
JQR	*Jewish Quarterly Review*
JQRMS	*Jewish Quarterly Review,* Monograph Series
JSOT	*Journal for the Study of the Old Testament*
JSOTSup	*Journal for the Study of the Old Testament,* Supplement Series
NRSV	New Revised Standard Version
NTS	*New Testament Studies*
PEQ	*Palestine Exploration Quarterly*
RB	*Revue biblique*
RechBib	Recherches bibliques
REJ	*Revue des études juives*
RevQ	*Revue de Qumran*
SBLRBS	SBL Resources for Biblical Study
SJLA	Studies in Judaism in Late Antiquity
SNTSMS	Society for New Testament Studies Monograph Series
STDJ	Studies on the Texts of the Desert of Judah
SUNT	Studien zur Umwelt des Neuen Testaments
SVTP	Studia in Veteris Testamenti pseudepigrapha
TRu	*Theologische Rundschau*
UTB	*Uni-Taschenbücher*
ZAW	*Zeitschrift für die alttestamentliche Wissenschaft*

Part I

THE DAMASCUS DOCUMENT FROM CAIRO AND QUMRAN

Editions, Translations, and Bibliographies

Editions of the Mediaeval Manuscripts of the Damascus Document

Baumgarten, J.M., and D.R. Schwartz with an appendix by Y. Ofer
 1995 'The Damascus Document (CD)', in J.H. Charlesworth with J.M. Baumgarten *et al.* (eds.), *The Dead Sea Scrolls: Hebrew, Aramaic, and Greek Texts
  with English Translations. Damascus Document, War Scroll, and Related Documents* (The Princeton Theological Seminary Dead Sea Scrolls Project, 2;
  Tübingen: J.C.B. Mohr [Paul Siebeck]; Louisville, KY: Westminster/John
  Knox Press): 4-57.
García Martínez, F., and E.J.C. Tigchelaar (eds.)
 1997 *The Dead Sea Scrolls Study Edition* (2 vols.; Leiden: E.J. Brill): I, 550-81.
Lohse, E.
 1986 *Die Texte aus Qumran* (Darmstadt: Wissenschaftliche Buchgesellschaft, 4th
  edn): 63-107.
Qimron, E.
 1992 'The Text of CDC', in M. Broshi (ed.), *The Damascus Document Reconsidered* (Jerusalem: Israel Exploration Society, The Shrine of the Book, Israel
  Museum): 9-49.
Rabin, C.
 1954 *The Zadokite Documents*. I. *The Admonition*. II. *The Laws* (Oxford: Clarendon).
 1958 *The Zadokite Documents*. I. *The Admonition*. II. *The Laws* (Oxford: Clarendon, rev. 2nd edn).
Rost, L.
 1933 *Die Damaskusschrift* (Kleine Texte für Vorlesungen und Übungen, 167;
  Berlin: De Gruyter).
Schechter, S.
 1910 *Documents of Jewish Sectaries*. I. *Fragments of a Zadokite Work* (Cambridge:
  Cambridge University Press).
Zeitlin, S.
 1952 *The Zadokite Fragments: Facsimile of the Manuscripts in the Cairo Genizah
  Collection in the Possession of the University Library, Cambridge, England*
  (JQRMS, 1; Philadelphia: Dropsie College).

Editions of the Qumran Fragments

Baillet, M., J.T. Milik, and R. de Vaux, OP
 1962 *Les 'Petites Grottes' de Qumrân: Exploration de la falaise, les grottes 2Q, 3Q, 5Q,*

6Q, 7Q à 10Q, le rouleau de cuivre (DJD, 3; Oxford: Clarendon): 128-31, 181.

Baumgarten, J.M., on the basis of transcriptions by J.T. Milik with contributions by S. Pfann and A. Yardeni

1996   *Qumran Cave 4. XIII. The Damascus Document (4Q266-273)* (DJD, 18; Oxford: Clarendon).

Baumgarten, J.M., with M.T. Davis

1995   'Cave IV, V, VI Fragments Related to the Damascus Document (4Q266-273 = 4QD^{a-h}, 5Q12 = 5QD, 6Q15 = 6QD', in J.H. Charlesworth with J.M. Baumgarten *et al.* (eds.), *The Dead Sea Scrolls. Hebrew, Aramaic, and Greek Texts with English Translations. Damascus Document, War Scroll, and Related Documents* (The Princeton Theological Seminary Dead Sea Scrolls Project, 2; Tübingen: J.C.B. Mohr [Paul Siebeck]; Louisville, KY: Westminster/John Knox Press): 59-79.

García Martínez, F., and E.J.C. Tigchelaar (eds.)

1997   *The Dead Sea Scrolls Study Edition* (2 vols.; Leiden: E.J. Brill): I, 581-627 [4QD].

1998   *The Dead Sea Scrolls Study Edition* (2 vols.; Leiden: E.J. Brill): II, 1134-35 [5QD], 1152-55 [6QD].

Stegemann, H.

1998b   'More Identified Fragments of *4QD^d (4Q269)*', *RevQ* 18: 497-509.

Tov, E., with the collaboration of S. Pfann (ed.).

1993   *The Dead Sea Scrolls on Microfiche: A Comprehensive Facsimile Edition of the Texts from the Judean Desert* (Leiden: E.J. Brill): final photos PAM 43.268-43.281 and 43.293-43.303 [4QD], 42.318 [5QD], 42.949 [6QD].

Wacholder, B.Z., and M.G. Abegg on the basis of the transcriptions of J.T. Milik and others (eds.)

1991   *A Preliminary Edition of the Unpublished Dead Sea Scrolls: The Hebrew and Aramaic Texts from Cave Four* (4 fascicles; Washington DC: Biblical Archaeology Society): I, 1-59.

Preliminary Descriptions of Cave 4 Fragments

Baumgarten, J.M.

1990   'The 4Q Zadokite Fragments on Skin Disease', *JJS* 41: 153-65.

1992a   'A New Qumran Substitute for the Divine Name and Mishnah Sukkah 4.5', *JQR* 83: 1-5.

1992b   'The Disqualifications of Priests in 4Q Fragments of the "Damascus Document", a Specimen of the Recovery of pre-Rabbinic Halakha', in J. Trebolle Barrera and L. Vegas Montaner (eds.), *The Madrid Qumran Congress: Proceedings of the International Congress on the Dead Sea Scrolls, Madrid 18–21 March 1991* (STDJ, 11; 2 vols.; Leiden: E.J. Brill): II, 503-13.

1992c   'A "Scriptural" Citation in 4Q Fragments of the Damascus Document', *JJS* 43: 95-98.

1992d   'The Cave 4 Versions of the Qumran Penal Code', *JJS* 43: 268-76.

1992e   'The Laws of the Damascus Document in Current Research', in M. Broshi
            (ed.), *The Damascus Document Reconsidered* (Jerusalem: Israel Exploration
            Society, The Shrine of the Book, Israel Museum): 51-62.

Milik, J.T.
    1959   *Ten Years of Discovery in the Wilderness of Judaea* (ET, J. Strugnell; London:
            SCM Press): 151-52.
    1966   'Fragment d'une source du Psautier (4QPs 89) et fragments des Jubilés, du
            Document de Damas, d'un Phylactère dans la Grotte 4 de Qumrân', *RB* 73:
            94-106, esp. 105 and Plate III.
    1972   'Milkî-ṣedeq et Milkî-rešaᶜ dans les anciens écrits juifs et chrétiens', *JJS* 23:
            95-144, esp. 135-36.
    1977   'Numérotation des feuilles des rouleaux dans le scriptorium de Qumrân',
            Semitica 27: 75-81, esp. 79-80 and Plate XI.

Milik, J.T. *et al.*
    1956   'Le travail d'édition des fragments manuscrits de Qumrân', *RB* 63: 49-67,
            esp. 61.

de Vaux, R., and J.T. Milik with contributions by J.W.B. Barns and J. Carswell
    1977   *Qumrân Grotte 4*. II (DJD, 6; Oxford: Clarendon): Plate IV.

Translations

Bardtke, H.
    1961   *Die Handschriftenfunde am Toten Meer: Die Sekte von Qumran* (Berlin:
            Evangelische Haupt-Bibelgesellschaft, 2nd edn): 259-76.

Baumgarten, J.M., and D.R. Schwartz
    1995   'Damascus Document (CD)', in J.H. Charlesworth with J.M. Baumgarten *et
            al.* (eds.), *The Dead Sea Scrolls. Hebrew, Aramaic, and Greek Texts with
            English Translations. Damascus Document, War Scroll, and Related Documents*
            (The Princeton Theological Seminary Dead Sea Scrolls Project, 2; Tübin-
            gen: J.C.B. Mohr [Paul Siebeck], Louisville, KY: Westminster/John Knox
            Press): 12-57, 64-79.

Burrows, M.
    1956   *The Dead Sea Scrolls* (London: Secker & Warburg): 349-64.

Charles, R.H.
    1977 (1913) *The Apocrypha and Pseudepigrapha of the Old Testament in English with
            Introductions and Critical and Explanatory Notes to the Several Books* (2 vols.;
            Oxford: Clarendon): II, 799-834. (The numeration of chapters and verses in
            this translation differs from that of the *editio princeps* by S. Schechter. The
            latter has been retained by most other scholars.).

Cook, E. in M. Wise, M. Abegg Jr., and E. Cook
    1996   *The Dead Sea Scrolls: A New Translation* (London: HarperCollins): 49-74.

Cothenet, É.
    1963   'Le Document de Damas', in J. Carmignac, É. Cothenet, and H. Lignée
            (eds.), *Les textes de Qumrân: Traduits et annotés* (2 vols.; Paris: Letouzey &
            Ané, 2nd edn): II, 149-204.

Davies, P.R.
    1983   *The Damascus Covenant: An Interpretation of the 'Damascus Document'*

(JSOTSup, 25; Sheffield: Sheffield Academic Press): 232-67 (Admonition only).

Dupont-Sommer, A.
1961   *The Essene Writings from Qumran* (ET, G. Vermes; Oxford: Blackwell): 121-63.

García Martínez, F.
1994   *The Dead Sea Scrolls Translated: The Qumran Texts in English* (ET, W.G.E. Watson; Leiden: E.J. Brill): 33- 71.

Gaster, T.H.
1957   *The Scriptures of the Dead Sea Sect in English Translation* (London: Secker & Warburg): 71-94.

Knibb, M.A.
1987   *The Qumran Community* (Cambridge Commentaries on Writings of the Jewish and Christian World 200 BC to AD 200; Cambridge: Cambridge University Press): 13-76 (Admonition only).

Lagrange, M.-J.
1912   'La secte juive de la Nouvelle Alliance au pays de Damas', *RB* NS 9: 213-40.

Lévi, I.
1911   'Un écrit sadducéen antérieur à la destruction du Temple', *REJ* 61: 161-205, esp. 172-205.

Lohse, E.
1986   *Die Texte aus Qumran* (Darmstadt: Wissenschaftliche Buchgesellschaft, 4th edn): 63-107.

Maier, J.
1995, 1996a *Die Qumran-Essener: Die Texte vom Toten Meer* (UTB, 1862–63; Basel: Friedrich Reinhardt), Volume I: 6-37; Volume II: 217-34.

Rabin, C.
1954   *The Zadokite Documents.* I. *The Admonition* II. *The Laws* (Oxford: Clarendon).
1958   *The Zadokite Documents.* I. *The Admonition* II. *The Laws* (Oxford: Clarendon, rev. 2nd edn).

Schechter, S.
1910   *Documents of Jewish Sectaries.* I. *Fragments of a Zadokite Work* (Cambridge: Cambridge University Press): xxxi-lvi.

Schwarz, O.J.R.
1965   *Der erste Teil der Damaskusschrift und das Alte Testament* (Diest: Lichtland): 3-66 (Admonition only).

Sutcliffe, E.F., SJ
1960   *The Monks of Qumran: The People of the Dead Sea Scrolls* (London: Burns & Oates): 131-48.

Vermes, G.
1997   *The Complete Dead Sea Scrolls in English* (London: Penguin Books): 125-53.

Bibliographies

Burchard, C.
1957   *Bibliographie zu den Handschriften vom Toten Meer* (BZAW, 76; Berlin: Töpelmann) [covers the period from 1948 to 1956].

1965   *Bibliographie zu den Handschriften vom Toten Meer*. II. *Nr. 1557-4459*
         (BZAW, 89; Berlin: Töpelmann) [covers the period from 1956 to 1962].
Fitzmyer, J.A., SJ
1970   Prolegomenon to the reprint of S. Schechter, *Documents of Jewish Sectaries*. I.
         Fragments of a Zadokite Work (New York: Ktav): 25-37.
1990   *The Dead Sea Scrolls: Major Publications and Tools for Study* (SBLRBS, 20;
         Atlanta: Scholars Press, rev. edn).
García Martínez, F.
1992   'Damascus Document: A Bibliography of Studies 1970–1989', in M. Broshi
         (ed.), *The Damascus Document Reconsidered* (Jerusalem: Israel Exploration
         Society, The Shrine of the Book, Israel Museum): 63–83.
García Martínez, F., and D.W. Parry
1996   *Bibliography of the Finds in the Desert of Judah 1970-1995* (STDJ, 19;
         Leiden: E.J. Brill).
García Martínez, F., and E.J.C. Tigchelaar
1998   'Bibliography of the Dead Sea Scrolls', *RevQ* 18: 459-90, 605-39.
Jongeling, B.
1971   *A Classified Bibliography of the Finds in the Desert of Judah 1958–1969*
         (STDJ, 7; Leiden: E.J. Brill).
LaSor, W.S.
1958   *Bibliography of the Dead Sea Scrolls 1948-1957* (Fuller Library Bulletin, 31;
         Pasadena, CA: Fuller Theological Seminary Library).
Maier, J.
1996b   *Die Qumran-Essener: Die Texte vom Toten Meer* (UTB, 1916; Basel: Friedrich
         Reinhardt): III, 378-477.
Pinnick, A.
         Weekly up-dated on-line bibliography of the Dead Sea Scrolls 1995 to the
         present, *The Orion Center for the Study of the Dead Sea Scrolls and Associated
         Literature Website:* http://orion.mscc.huji.ac.il

1

INTRODUCTION

1. A Tale of Two Discoveries: Cairo and Qumran

The Damascus Document constitutes something of a special case among the Dead Sea Scrolls. Whereas the contents of the Qumran caves were discovered in the 1940s and 1950s, the Damascus Document was already known to scholars from the end of the nineteenth century. Two manuscripts of the Damascus Document reached the world of scholarship from the storeroom of a synagogue in Old Cairo known as the Cairo *genizah*. A *genizah* is a storeroom attached to synagogues in which all kinds of documents, both hand-written and printed, are kept prior to their disposal by burial in consecrated ground. Documents might be kept in a *genizah* in order to preserve them from improper use. Under normal circumstances the contents of these storerooms would in time be disposed of and never reach posterity. Fortunately for scholars of Jewish history the contents of the Cairo *genizah* were forgotten or for other unknown reasons survived. The Damascus Document is only one of the texts recovered from the Cairo *genizah,* which revealed amongst many other works copies of the Wisdom of Ben Sira in the original Hebrew.

Two mediaeval copies of the Damascus Document were brought back from Cairo to England by the Cambridge Talmud scholar Solomon Schechter. Schechter's journey to Cairo was supported by Charles Taylor, then Master of St John's College, Cambridge. Schechter and Taylor donated both manuscripts to the Cambridge University Library where they are kept to this day. Schechter published the first edition of the Damascus Document in 1910 under the title *Fragments of a Zadokite Work*. This title was chosen because the community behind parts of the document seems to refer to itself as 'the sons of Zadok', cf. for example CD 3.20b–4.4a. The title that is most commonly used today, the Damascus Document (abbreviated CD which stands for 'Cairo Damascus

Document'), is based on several references to 'the land of Damascus' or 'Damascus' in the first part of the document, cf. for example CD 6.5, 19; 7.15, 19; 8.21; 19.34; 20.12.

The two mediaeval manuscripts from Cairo are usually referred to as manuscript A and manuscript B. Manuscript A is the longer and older of the two manuscripts. It contains 16 pages and dates from the tenth century CE. Its contents can be divided into an Admonition (pages 1-8) and a collection of Laws (pages 9-16). Manuscript B dates from the twelfth century CE and consists of two pages which partly overlap with manuscript A. The original editor of the document introduced the numbers 19 and 20 to refer to the two pages of manuscript B. Page 19 contains a different version of pages 7 and 8 from manuscript A, and page 20 contains additional material which constitutes the end of the Admonition as it is known from the Cairo text. We will look at the differences between both manuscripts in more detail in Chapter 7 below. The contents of CD can be clearly divided into a section of Laws (CD 9–16) and an Admonition (CD 1–8; 19–20).

After the Dead Sea Scrolls were found in what would eventually amount to 11 caves near the western shore of the Dead Sea, scholars soon recognized a connection between the Damascus Document and those discoveries. Such a connection was indicated first by the occurrence in the Biblical Commentaries from Qumran of the nicknames 'teacher of righteousness' and 'spouter of lies' known hitherto only from the Damascus Document. Secondly, a number of similarities in ideology, vocabulary, and organization were recognized. Finally, the discovery of ancient fragments of the Damascus Document in Caves 4, 5, and 6 of Qumran proved those scholars right who had argued that the mediaeval manuscripts were based on a much older original. Since the discovery of fragments of the Damascus Document at Qumran, the document is universally taken as part of the Qumran library and studied in this context. The existence of fragments of the Damascus Document at Qumran was taken to indicate, moreover, that the work had been composed by the community responsible for the *pesharim* (a type of Biblical Commentary attested at Qumran) and other sectarian works. More recently the place of the Damascus Document at Qumran and its relationship to other Qumran texts have become subjects of scholarly debate.

Fragments of the Damascus Document were found in Qumran Caves 4, 5, and 6 (4QD, 5QD, 6QD). The material from Caves 5 and 6 consists of a small amount of text only and was published as early as 1962 by J.T. Milik and M. Baillet. Qumran Cave 4, on the other hand, yielded a rich and significant amount of fragments belonging to the Damascus Document. In all, eight manuscripts of this document were found in Cave

4, and these have recently been published by J.M. Baumgarten. A considerable proportion of 4QD is paralleled by the text of CD with minor variations. However, the Cave 4 manuscripts reveal some exhortatory and a significant amount of legal material that is not attested in CD.

The legal part of the Damascus Document has been somewhat neglected in Qumran studies to date. A notable exception is the work of L. Ginzberg in his study *An Unknown Jewish Sect* (1976 [orig. 1922]). Scholars tended to devote their attention chiefly to the Admonition. With the recent publication of 4QD it has become clear that the work as a whole is primarily a legal work, and the legal part of the document is likely to receive more attention in the years to come.

2. How Did the Damascus Document Get to Cairo?

The proper context for the scholarly study of the Damascus Document is, as we saw, as part of the Qumran library. This leaves us with the task of attempting to explain how mediaeval copies of this ancient text came to be deposited in a synagogue in Cairo. The most likely explanation draws on a report of an earlier manuscript discovery in the vicinity of Qumran. A letter to Sergius, the Metropolitan of Elam, by the Nestorian Patriarch of Seleucia Timotheus I (726–819 CE) written around 800 CE mentions reports of a discovery of books in a cave near Jericho some ten years previously. The report then recounts that the Arab discoverer of the cave notified the Jews of Jerusalem who retrieved several books of the Hebrew Bible as well as other books written in Hebrew. It seems probable that an ancient copy of the Damascus Document was among these books, that mediaeval copies of the work were produced subsequently, and that at least two of these reached the Jewish community in Cairo and ended up in the *genizah*. H. Stegemann has proposed that the cave from which the ancient copy of the Damascus Document was taken was Qumran Cave 3, because on its discovery by archaeologists this cave showed clear traces of an earlier discovery (1998a: 68-71). An ingenious hypothesis that is, however, impossible to verify.

Further Reading

On the Cairo Genizah

Kahle, P.
1959   *The Cairo Genizah* (Oxford: Blackwell, 2nd edn). This is the second edition of Kahle's classic work on the Cairo *genizah*. The first edition appeared

before the discovery of the Dead Sea Scrolls, and Kahle revised his book in the light of these new momentous discoveries. Especially the first chapter provides an immensely readable account of the discovery of the *genizah* and subsequent events.

Reif, S.

2000   'Cairo Genizah', in L.H. Schiffman and J.C. VanderKam (eds.), *Encyclopedia of the Dead Sea Scrolls* (2 vols.; New York: Oxford University Press): I, 105-108.

http://www.lib.cam.ac.uk/Taylor-Schechter

The website of the Cambridge University Library Taylor-Schechter Collection which holds the bulk of the Cairo Genizah finds, including the Damascus Document.

On the supposed 'Zadokite character' of the Damascus Document

Davies, P.R.

1987   *Behind the Essenes: History and Ideology in the Dead Sea Scrolls* (BJS, 94; Atlanta: Scholars Press): 51-72. Davies offers a critical discussion that emphasizes the lack of evidence for an identification of a Zadokite group behind the document. Recently important new evidence on the place of 'the sons of Zadok' in the scrolls has come to light from the Cave 4 manuscripts of the Community Rule. For details, compare S. Metso's volume (*Serekh*, forthcoming) in this series.

On the classical evidence on the Essenes

Beall, T.S.

1988   *Josephus' Description of the Essenes Illustrated by the Dead Sea Scrolls* (SNTSMS, 58; Cambridge: Cambridge University Press).

Bergmeier, R.

1993   *Die Essener-Berichte des Flavius Josephus: Quellenstudien zu den Essenertexten im Werk des Jüdischen Historiographen* (Kampen: Kok Pharos).

Bilde, P.

1998   'The Essenes in Philo and Josephus', in F.H. Cryer and T.L. Thompson (eds.), *Qumran Between the Old and New Testaments* (Copenhagen International Seminar, 6; JSOTSup, 290; Sheffield: Sheffield Academic Press): 32-68.

Vermes G., and M.D. Goodman

1989   *The Essenes: According to the Classical Sources* (Oxford Centre Textbooks, 1; Sheffield: JSOT Press).

On the history of scholarship on the Damascus Document

Davies, P.R.

1983   *The Damascus Covenant: An Interpretation of the 'Damascus Document'* (JSOTSup, 25; Sheffield: Sheffield Academic Press): 1-47.

On earlier manuscript discoveries in caves

Rowley, H.H.

1952   *The Zadokite Fragments and the Dead Sea Scrolls* (Oxford: Blackwell): 21-30.

2

PHYSICAL DESCRIPTION OF THE MANUSCRIPTS

1. Cairo Damascus Document

As we saw, two manuscripts of the Damascus Document have been discovered in the Cairo *genizah*. Manuscript A comprises 16 pages (CD 1–
16) written on both sides of eight sheets of paper and dates from the tenth
century CE. The customary numbering of the pages of manuscript A goes
back to Schechter's *editio princeps*. However, the ordering of the pages of
the legal part (CD 9–16) has since been altered. Two Cave 4 manuscripts
(i.e. 4QD^a 8 i-ii and 4QD^e 6 i-iii) clearly indicate that the contents of pages
15-16 immediately precede the beginning of the material found in CD 9,
and J.T. Milik, the member of the original editorial team working on
4QD, announced this reversal of the order of pages 15-16 in the 1950s
(1959: 151-52). Thus, according to this adjustment manuscript A comprises the Admonition in CD 1–8 and Laws in CD 15–16 and CD 9–14
in that order. This corrected sequence is reflected in the recent edition of
CD by Baumgarten and Schwartz whereas Qimron's edition retains the
original sequence of the pages. CD 1.1 begins with a vacat, and it is impossible to say with certainty whether this constituted the beginning of the
mediaeval copy or whether one or several pages are missing at the beginning. In terms of content the material that opens CD 1 constitutes a suitable opening for the work. However, we will see below that some of the
Cave 4 manuscripts contain additional material preceding the equivalent
of CD 1.1. CD 8, the end of the Admonition in manuscript A, breaks off
abruptly at the bottom of the page with no indication that we have come
to the end of a section. The legal part begins in CD 15.1 in the middle
of a sentence, and manuscript A again breaks off abruptly at the end of
CD 14. The Admonition (CD 1–8) regularly comprises 21 lines per page
whereas the legal part (CD 9–16) comprises 23 lines per page in those

cases where the bottom of the page is preserved. The lower parts of CD 13–16 are badly damaged, and the number of lines is only clearly preserved in CD 9–12.

Manuscript B dates from the twelfth century CE and comprises two pages (CD 19–20) that partly overlap with manuscript A although both texts contain significant variants in the overlapping sections. CD 20 is written on the back of the same sheet as CD 19. Manuscript B begins in the middle of a sentence in CD 19.1. It is difficult to be sure whether the end of CD 20 constituted the end of manuscript B in which case this manuscript would have lacked the legal part altogether. In favour of this view Rabin has noted that page 20 has only 34 lines in contrast to CD 19 with 35 lines (1954: 43). However, within a sample of two pages only the difference of one line is not substantial enough to make a strong case. Moreover, if manuscript B contained additional text the addition of a further line on page 20 would have resulted in a smaller bottom margin than we would expect on the basis of CD 19. CD 19 has a bottom margin of 2.0-2.2 cm whereas the bottom margin of CD 20 measures 2.2-2.5 cm. Any additional lines at the end of CD 20 would have resulted in a margin of approximately 1.2-1.8 cm. Finally, a number of scholars have observed that the expression 'these laws' in CD 20.27b refers forward to the legal part of the document which seems the most natural understanding of that phrase. In the absence of further evidence it is impossible to achieve certainty but on balance it seems doubtful that manuscript B did not include a legal part. Finally, 4QD^a 4.9, 11-13 preserves the fragmentary remains of a number of additional lines that seem to continue the blessing beyond CD 20.33-34. It is open to question, therefore, whether CD 20.34 constitutes the end of the Admonition in manuscript B and whether further admonitory material would have followed at the top of another page that has not survived.

Both manuscripts are unpointed with the exception of a number of words that have been vocalized using both the Babylonian and the Tiberian system of vocalization (Y. Ofer in Charlesworth *et al.* 1995: 10-11).

2. Parchment Cairo Fragment

A number of scholars have identified a further fragment related to the Damascus Document from the Cairo Genizah. This small parchment fragment (pergCfr) contains the remains of nine lines and was first published by I. Lévi in 1913. Lévi (1913) argued that the fragment is a tenth-century CE autograph written by a member of the Zadokites responsible for CD over a century previously. More recently, J. Fitzmyer concurred with the view that the fragment is related to the Damascus Document (1970: 14). The text of this fragment, which includes a reference to 'the congregation of the sons of Zadok' in line 3, does not, however, overlap with any of the mediaeval or ancient copies of the Damascus Document. As Lévi has observed, the top and bottom of the fragment are blank and the piece does not appear to belong to a larger work. Its exact relationship to CD is difficult to establish with certainty except to say that it was found in the same hoard of mediaeval manuscripts and shares some of its terminology.

3. The Cave 4 Manuscripts

With the exception of 4QD^h (4Q273), which is written on papyrus, all the remaining Cave 4 manuscripts are written on parchment. Students need to be aware that a change of sigla has occurred in the case of the majority of the Cave 4 manuscripts and that some publications use different sigla to what is now the standard. Where applicable I have added the older siglum in parentheses.

4QD^a (4Q266 *olim* 4QD^b) constitutes the oldest and most extensive manuscript of the Damascus Document from Cave 4. In the official edition this manuscript comprises 11 numbered and identified fragments and a further 64 numbered and unidentified fragments. The latter are largely very small indeed with no more than traces of letters. The numbered and identified fragments, by contrast, frequently comprise numerous individual fragments grouped together and often extend over several columns. The fragmentary opening column of 4QD^a with a fastening device still attached has been preserved as well as the fragmentary closing column followed by an empty handle sheet. Thus, 4QD^a preserves both the beginning and the end of the document. The script has been dated to the first half of the first century BCE. G.J. Brooke advises caution, however, and prefers to be no more specific than the end of the first century for the date of 4QD^a—referred to under its earlier siglum 4QD^b in his article—(1991: 215-16). 4QD^a was one of the second batch of manuscripts submitted to AMS (Accelerator Mass Spectrometry) C-14 dating recently, which resulted in dates in the region of 5–80 CE (1σ) and 45 BCE–120 CE (2σ). In this manuscript the divine name *el* is written in square script.

4QD^b (4Q267 *olim* 4QD^d) comprises nine numbered identified fragments and nine unidentified fragments. In this manuscript the divine name *el* is found written in square script, cf. 4QD^b 2.5, 7, 13; 9 iv 11, alongside instances where it is written in Palaeo-Hebrew (a more ancient Hebrew script), cf. 4QD^b 3.7; 9 i 2; 9 iv 4, and 9 v 4. 4QD^b has been dated to the end of the first century BCE or the beginning of the first century CE on the basis of its script, and A. Yardeni has proposed that it might have been copied by the same scribe as 4QMMT^d (4Q397) (A. Yardeni in Baumgarten 1996: 96). This manuscript also underwent recent C-14 tests resulting in a date of 172–98 BCE (1σ) and 194–45 BCE (2σ). Fragment 1 preserves traces of horizontal dry lines.

4QD^c (4Q268 *olim* 4QD^a) is made up of three fragments only and has been given a palaeographical date around the middle of the first century CE. The divine name *el* is written in Palaeo-Hebrew in this manuscript. Remnants of horizontal dry lines are preserved.

4QD^d (4Q269 *olim* 4QD^f) includes 14 numbered fragments in the DJD edition by J.M. Baumgarten and has been dated to the end of the first century BCE on the basis of its script. Most recently H. Stegemann has published two further fragments of this manuscript, one of which preserves part of the final column of text (1998b; see also Tigchelaar 1999). In this manuscript the divine name *el* is written in square script. Traces of horizontal and vertical dry lines are preserved.

4QD^e (4Q270) constitutes the second largest 4QD manuscript and comprises seven numbered identified fragments as well as five numbered unidentified fragments. The script has been dated to the first half of the first century CE. The divine name *el* is written in square script. The manuscript clearly preserves horizontal and vertical lines. Distinctively among the 4QD manuscripts 4QD^e 3 i 19 contains writing in red ink. The traces of letters written in red ink are only faintly preserved and difficult to decipher. The editor has proposed reading and restoring '[Concerning] the sta[tutes of the] lands'. 4QD^e 7 ii preserves the end of the work as is clearly indicated by the presence of several empty ruled lines at the end of the column followed by another empty ruled column to the left.

4QD^f (4Q271 *olim* 4QD^c) includes five numbered fragments. Fine traces of vertical and horizontal lines are preserved, and the divine name *el* is written in square script. The script has been dated to the beginning of the second half of the first century BCE.

4QDᵍ (4Q272) comprises two columns of one identified fragment and the scant remains of two unidentified fragments. The palaeographical date suggested for this manuscript is towards the end of the first century BCE.

4QpapDʰ (4Q273) is a poorly preserved papyrus manuscript comprising six numbered identified fragments and three unidentified fragments. The script has been dated to the end of the first century BCE.

4. 5QD (5Q12)

Only one leather fragment with remnants of five lines has been preserved of this manuscript. The editor proposed a palaeographical date in the second half of the first century BCE.

5. 6QD (6Q15)

Five leather fragments of this manuscript have been preserved. Traces of horizontal lines are visible, and the editor dated the script to the first century CE.

In sum, all ten ancient copies of the Damascus Document originated in the time spanning from the beginning of the first century BCE to the middle of the first century CE. This period corresponds more or less to the period of occupation of the Qumran settlement. The evidence of the coins uncovered on the site suggests a date around 100 BCE for the beginning of occupation in the Second Temple period (Laperrousaz 1976: 29-33), and the site was abandoned around 68 CE when it fell into the hands of the Roman army. There is no reason to believe that any of the ancient manuscripts of D constitute autographs, and the date of the document's composition needs to be distinguished from the date of the copies. The Damascus Document in its final form was probably composed towards the end of the second century BCE since CD 19.35b–20.1a; 20.13b-15a presuppose the death of the teacher of righteousness. According to CD 1 this figure is associated with the early history of a community around the middle of the second century BCE. In any case the document must have been in existence before its earliest copy 4QDᵃ was produced in the first half of the first century BCE.

An important question that needs to be addressed is the relationship of the shorter mediaeval Cairo text to the longer Cave 4 versions of the document. The editor of 4QD frequently speaks of CD 'omitting' or 'abbreviating' the longer text as attested in the Cave 4 manuscripts (Baumgarten 1996: 45, 75). A comparable assessment is found in the revised third edition of G. Vermes's introduction to the scrolls (1994: 44). However, on the basis of the available evidence it is preferable to speak in more objective terms of CD's 'shorter text' or of CD 'lacking' a particular passage since the statement that CD 'omits' material present in 4QD needs to be argued for rather than asserted. Two pioneers in the study of the Damascus Document, S. Schechter (1910: ix) and L. Rost (1933: 1), have commented on the incomplete and fragmentary character of the mediaeval text. Moreover, elsewhere Schechter speaks of his impression that the mediaeval manuscripts preserve 'extracts from a larger work', a notion that is reflected in the choice of title for his *editio princeps* (1910: x). Side by side with references to the omission of additional material in CD Baumgarten himself has elsewhere reflected more cautiously on the relationship between the mediaeval and the ancient copies of the document (1996: 6-7).

For a number of reasons it seems plausible to think of CD's shorter text as having emerged accidentally rather than as a result of a deliberate editorial process. Firstly, we note the scarcity of significant variants in the material preserved both in CD and 4QD. It seems unlikely that CD's text should display such a close relationship to the text of the 4QD manuscripts where both overlap and at the same time begin to diverge radically in those places where CD's text has not survived. Moreover, a look at those places in the mediaeval copies of the Damascus Document where the missing material would be expected to occur is revealing. CD 1.1 begins with an indentation. The equivalent material in 4QDᵃ 2 i 6 and 4QDᶜ 1.8-9 is similarly set apart from what precedes as a new section marked by a vacat. CD 3 and 9 both begin with indentations, and it is therefore questionable that CD 1 constitutes the first page of the mediaeval manuscript. Manuscript A breaks off abruptly and clearly in mid-flow just after the beginning of the penal code in CD 14. There is thus no way of knowing where the text of manuscript A ended, and there is no positive evidence to suggest that it diverged from the material that follows in the 4QD manuscripts. The missing portion of additional legal material between the Admonition and the Laws in CD can equally be explained as having arisen as a consequence of accidental loss since the legal part in CD begins in CD 15.1 apparently in the middle of a sentence. Finally, it is noteworthy that no ancient copy corresponds to the shorter text of CD. In sum, CD's shorter text can be explained as having emerged as a result of accidental loss and there is no need to postulate a deliberate process of omission and abbreviation, although on the basis of the evidence we cannot dismiss the latter as a possibility.

Further Reading

On the physical and palaeographical description of the manuscripts

Baillet, M., J.T. Milik, and R. de Vaux, OP

  1962   *Les 'Petites Grottes' de Qumrân: Exploration de la falaise, les grottes 2Q, 3Q, 5Q, 6Q, 7Q à 10Q, le rouleau de cuivre* (DJD, 3; Oxford: Clarendon): 128-31 (for 6QD) and 181 (for 5QD).

Baumgarten, J.M., on the basis of transcriptions by J.T. Milik with contributions by S. Pfann and A. Yardeni

  1996   *Qumran Cave 4. XIII. The Damascus Document (4Q266-273)* (DJD, 18; Oxford: Clarendon). The contributions containing the physical and palaeographical descriptions of the manuscripts go back to S. Pfann and A. Yardeni respectively.

Brooke, G.J.

  1991   'The Messiah of Aaron in the Damascus Document', *RevQ* 15: 215-30.

Schechter, S.

  1910   *Documents of Jewish Sectaries*. I. *Fragments of a Zadokite Work* (Cambridge: Cambridge University Press): ix-xi for a description of the two mediaeval manuscripts of CD.

On the radiocarbon tests of 4QD manuscripts

Jull, A.T.T., D.J. Donahue, M. Broshi, and E. Tov

  1996   'Radiocarbon Dating of Scrolls and Linen Fragments from the Judean Desert', *ᶜAtiqot* 28: 1-7.

On a recently identified fragment of 4QD[d]

Stegemann, H.

  1998b   'More Identified Fragments of *4QD[d] (4Q269)*', *RevQ* 18: 497-509.

On the date of the composition of the Damascus Document

Knibb, M.A.

  1994   'The Place of the Damascus Document', in M.O. Wise, N. Golb, J.J. Collins, and D.G. Pardee (eds.), *Methods of Investigation of the Dead Sea Scrolls and the Khirbet Qumran Site: Present Realities and Future Prospects* (ANYAS, 722; New York: New York Academy of Sciences): 149-62.

3

OUTLINE OF THE CONTENTS OF THE DAMASCUS
MANUSCRIPTS FROM CAIRO AND QUMRAN

In what follows I will provide an outline of the contents of the Damascus Document manuscripts from Cairo and Qumran. In compiling this outline I was able to draw upon the recently published outline by J.M. Baumgarten (Baumgarten in Charlesworth *et al.* 1995: 5) as well as his earlier description of the contents of the Laws (1992e). As far as the arrangement of the additional material provided by the Cave 4 fragments is concerned Baumgarten has built upon J.T. Milik's earlier arrangement (Baumgarten 1996: 2-3). Hartmut Stegemann and his assistants Annette Steudel and Alexander Maurer of the University of Göttingen in Germany have worked on the material reconstruction of the Cave 4 fragments over the course of many years, and Stegemann has recently presented the status quo of his results in public at a symposium celebrating the centenary of research on the Damascus Document at the Hebrew University in Jerusalem (Stegemann 2000). It is possible that modifications to the sequence of some of the Cave 4 fragments as arranged in Baumgarten's edition will be developed in the light of future research. In the outline given below I follow the arrangement offered by Milik and Baumgarten. No attempt has been made to list all the variants between various manuscripts of the document although I have attempted to refer to all significant variants.

The Opening Lines of the Damascus Document
(4QD^a 1 a-b.1-5a)
4QD^a 1 a-b.1-5a preserves the opening lines of the Damascus Document. This is clear from the preservation of a fastening device and a wide right margin (Baumgarten 1996: Plate I). Unfortunately the opening words have not survived. In the preserved text the sons of light are admonished to

keep separate from undesirable ways until the time of the visitation has been completed.

An Admonition Preceding the Beginning of the Cairo Text
(4QD^a 1 a-b.5b-25; 1 c-f ?; 2 i 1-6a; 4QD^b 1.2-8; 4QD^c 1.1-8)

Following the opening lines of D as fragmentarily preserved in 4QD^a and immediately preceding the beginning of the Cairo text (CD 1.1), 4QD^{a-c} provide a substantial amount of additional text, approximately one column of 24–25 lines of 4QD^a's text. This additional material begins in 4QD^a 1 a-b.5 with a partially preserved call to hearken ('[And now listen] to me and I will make known to you...') of the type found also in CD 1.1 par. 4QD^a 2 i 6 and 4QD^c 1.9; CD 2.2 par. 4QD^a 2 ii 2; CD 2.14 par. 4QD^a 2 ii 13-14; 4QD^e 2 ii 19. The lines that follow refer to the correct observance of appointed times and repeatedly emphasize the importance of divinely ordained time schemes, they admonish those who seek God's commandments to walk in perfect ways and refer to a revelation of hidden things. The group of fragments numbered 4QD^a 1 c-f may preserve further material belonging to this exhortatory section although their placement is uncertain (Baumgarten 1996: 33-34 and Plate I).

First Description of the Origins of a Movement
(CD 1.1–2.1; 4QD^a 2 i 6b-24; 4QD^c 1.9-17)

This section constitutes the beginning of the Damascus Document as preserved in the Cairo text. A new section seems to begin at this point in the Qumran manuscripts of D as well since both 4QD^a 2 i 6 and 4QD^c 1.8-9 leave some blank space before preserving the opening words of CD 1. Following a call for attention and the announcement of God's dispute with all flesh CD 1.3-12 par. contains a description of the divine punishment inflicted upon Israel with the exile followed by the preservation of a remnant and the emergence of a movement. The new movement is said to have been brought about through divine intervention 390 years after the people's deliverance into the hand of the Babylonian king Nebuchadnezzar. The text goes on to say that for a 20-year period the new movement lacked direction until God raised a teacher of righteousness to provide guidance. CD 1.13–2.1 par. consists of a polemical description of a group referred to as 'the congregation of traitors'. In CD 1.13-18 par. this group is described as having been led astray by an individual referred to as 'the scoffer who dripped waters of lies over Israel', and one gets the impression that the expression 'the congregation of traitors' is applied to a contemporary rival group. In CD 1.19–2.1 par. the disregard of the congregation of traitors for the correct observance of the law and their hatred of those who behave with righteousness are emphasized. In these lines the authors

seem to have in mind both pre-exilic Israel as well as contemporary opponents of the group behind D (Knibb 1987: 23-25).

God's Dealings with the Righteous and the Wicked Followed by a Second Description of the Origins of a Movement
(CD 2.2-13; 4QDᵃ 2 ii 1-13a)

A second call for attention addressed to all those entering the covenant
introduces this section. The Hebrew expression can be taken to mean 'all
those entering the covenant' or 'all the members of the covenant' (Davies
1983: 72). This is followed by a dualistic exposition of God's dealings
with the righteous and the wicked. Whereas the righteous can expect expiation, the fate of the wicked lies in destruction. CD 2.7b-10 par. is characterized by a strongly deterministic outlook. God knew the deeds of hu-
mans before their creation. CD 2.11-13 par. comprises a second description of the origins of a movement which shares a number of elements with
the first description in CD 1.3-12 par. referred to above (Hempel 1999).
However, in contrast to the latter description the present passage lacks the
reference to the teacher of righteousness. Instead here the prophets, 'those
anointed with his holy spirit and the seers of truth', provide instruction to
the newly formed movement. 4QDᵃ 2 ii 3 contains the three additional
words 'from all the paths of sin' not present in CD 2.3.

Exhortation Spelling out the Consequences of Following Guilty Thoughts and Lustful eyes
(CD 2.14–3.12a; 4QDᵃ 2 ii 14-23; iii 5, 19-20; 4QDᵉ 1 i 1-3)

A third call for attention introduces this section. Those addressed are in-
structed to understand the deeds of God so that they may choose that
which pleases God and reject that which he hates. The bulk of this section
recalls how past generations brought divine punishment upon themselves
by following guilty thoughts and lustful eyes from the generation of the
watchers (cf. Gen. 6.1-4) to the exile. Only three faithful individuals (Abraham, Isaac, and Jacob) are singled out as obedient and worthy of the description 'friends of God'. Very little is preserved of 4QDᵉ 1 i 3, but this
manuscript seems to lack the words 'when they walked in the hardness of
their hearts they [i.e. the watchers] fell' (Baumgarten 1996: 141).

Third Description of the Origins of a Movement
(CD 3.12b–4.12a; 4QDᵃ 3 i 1-5; 4QDᵉ 1 ii a-b)

This passage comprises a third description of the origins of a movement in
the Damascus Document and can be divided into a number of sub-sec-
tions. According to CD 3.12b-17a the movement originated with a righteous remnant after the exile. The establishment of the movement is here

described in terms of an everlasting covenant. A key event in the description of the formation of the movement is the reference to a divine revelation of hidden things in which all Israel had gone astray. This revelation comprises what is described in general terms as knowledge of God's will and is further said to have disclosed calendrical matters. The correct observance of the calendar was obviously an issue of considerable importance to the author of this passage. CD 3.17b-20b describes the origins of a movement in terms of divine expiation for transgressions and the establishment of a 'sure house'. The latter expression constitutes an allusion to the promise of a priestly dynasty to Zadok in 1 Sam. 2.35. CD 3.20c–4.4a contains a quotation and interpretation of Ezek. 44.15. The quotation from Ezekiel differs significantly from the Masoretic text. Whereas the Masoretic text of Ezek. 44.15 speaks of one group ('the levitical priests, the descendants of Zadok' in the rendering of the NRSV), the verse as quoted in the Damascus Document mentions three groups: the priests, the levites, and the sons of Zadok. The interpretation that follows identifies each of these groups with the members of the new movement in three phases of its existence. The priests are described as 'the converts of Israel who went out from the land of Judah', the levites are identified as those who joined them, and the sons of Zadok as the elect of Israel at the end of days. The Hebrew expression translated here with 'the converts of Israel' has been translated differently by some scholars. Two alternative translations are possible: 'the returnees of Israel' or 'the captivity of Israel'. We will return to the meaning of this expression in Chapter 5 below. The phrase 'the end of days' is often taken to refer to the time in which the author of this passage thought himself to be living. The interpretation of CD 4.4b-12a par. is made difficult by two factors. First, the text resumes after the interpretation of Ezek. 44.15 with the announcement of a list of names and other details about the individuals included, but no such list follows. Secondly, after the lacuna, which presumably at some point incorporated the lost list, the text is corrupt, which makes it very difficult to grasp the meaning of the rest of this section with certainty. Unfortunately the group of fragments labelled 4QD^a 3 i that parallel part of this section are very fragmentary and their preserved text sets in just after the textually difficult passage in CD 4.4b-6. The passage refers back to the first members of the movement as well as subsequent generations of members. The material expresses strongly deterministic views and seems to be intended to urge those addressed to join the movement before it is too late. The passage takes up again the theme of God's forgiveness for sins which was stressed in CD 3.17b-20b above. A new element introduced here in connection with the emergence of a new movement is the emphasis on the correct interpretation of the law received by the first members of the movement, cf. CD 4.8 par.

Israel under the Dominion of Belial
(CD 4.12b–5.19; 4QD^a 3 i 6-7; ii 1-7a; 4QD^b 2.1-3; 6QD 1.1-3; 2.1-2; 3.1-2)
Whereas much of the preceding material in the Admonition focused on Israel's past shortcomings and the resulting consequences, the present section turns to contemporary society. In the author's view contemporary society is under the dominion of Belial, the ruler of the forces of wickedness (Knibb 1987: 40). Based on an interpretation of Isa. 24.17 it is argued that Israel is ensnared by 'the three nets of Belial' which are identified as fornication, wealth, and polluting the sanctuary. CD 4.19b–5.11a contains a commentary on the interpretation of Isa. 24.17 which focuses on what the author regards as prevalent sexual malpractices in society. This commentary relates somewhat awkwardly to what precedes. It has been argued that CD 4.12b–5.19 is not of one piece but is made up from separate sources and secondary expansions (Davies 1983: 108-19). CD 5.11b-19 par. condemns the author's opponents for failing to obey the statutes of the covenant and reminds those addressed of Israel's shortcomings in the past. This section closes in CD 5.17b-19 with a retrospective note referring to the period of the exodus when Moses and Aaron where raised up by God whereas Jannes and Jambres where raised up by Belial to oppose the former pair. In later Jewish tradition Jannes and Jambres are the names given to the Egyptian magicians competing with Moses according to Exod. 7.11 (Knibb 1987: 46). In this context both 4QD^a 3 ii 6 and 4QD^b 2.2 attest the reading 'when Israel acted wickedly for the first time', presumably an allusion to the golden-calf incident (cf. Exod. 32), whereas CD 5.19 reads 'when Israel was saved for the first time'. J. Duhaime has argued for the presence of a number of dualistic reworkings in the scrolls, and has identified CD 5.17b-19 as such a reworking in the Damascus Document (1987: 51-55).

A Fourth Description of the Origins of a Movement
(CD 5.20–6.11a; 4QD^a 3 ii 7b-13; 4QD^b 2.4-15; 4QD^d 4 i 1-3; 6QD 3.2-5)
This fourth account of the origins of a movement is again closely linked to the time of the exile. At the core of this account lies a midrashic interpretation of Num. 21.18 in which the well of the Numbers passage is identified as the law. Unlike CD 6.3 both 4QD^a 3 ii 10 and 4QD^b 2.9 preface the citation of Num. 21.18 with the introductory formula 'as Moses said'. This section is customarily referred to as 'the Well midrash'. Those who dig the well are identified with 'the converts (or returnees) of Israel who went out from the land of Judah and sojourned in the land of Damascus'. The sceptre is identified with an individual described as 'the

interpreter of the law' who is said to provide guidance to the movement until the end of days which will see the arrival of 'the one who will teach righteousness' (CD 6.11). It has been argued by some that this midrash existed independently before its incorporation into the Admonition (Davies 1983: 119-25; see also Knibb 1987: 47).

A Prohibition on Participating in the Sacrificial Cult
(CD 6.11b-14a; 4QD[a] 3 ii 17b-19)
This passage prohibits members of the covenant community from participating in the sacrificial cult. Such a prohibition contrasts sharply with numerous statements in the legal part of the document that take participation in the temple cult for granted, cf. CD 16.13-17 par.; 9.13-14 par.; 11.17-21 par.; 4QD[a] 5 ii par.; 6 ii par.; 4QD[f] 2 par. It seems likely that the present passage goes back to a time when the community responsible for the Damascus Document in its final form had distanced itself from the contemporary temple administration. A critical attitude to the sacrificial cult is found in a number of documents from Qumran, cf. 1QS 3.11par.; 8.5b-6a, 8b-10a par.; 9.3-5 par. and 1QpHab 12.7-9.

A Series of Halakhic Rules Followed by a Promise and a Series of Warnings
(CD 6.14b–8.21a; CD 19.1-33a; 4QD[a] 3 ii 20-24; iii 4-6, 17-25; iv 1-6; 4QD[d] 4 ii 1-7; 6.1-2; 6QD 4.1-4)
An exhortation admonishing those addressed to conduct themselves according to a particular interpretation of the law ordained for the time of wickedness introduces this section. Twelve specific prescriptions follow, most of which are dealt with at greater length in the legal part of the document (Davies 1983: 161-62). Davies counts 13 prescriptions since on his analysis CD 6.11b-14 is part of the list of specific injunctions (Davies 1983: 125-42). This list of prescriptions is followed by a promise to those who observe these rulings and a warning addressed to those who fail to do so. Manuscript B picks up in the middle of the promise and provides a parallel account to manuscript A with significant differences. Somewhat out of place and separating the promise from the warning is an important statement endorsing marriage and family life for those who 'live in camps according to the rule of the land' (Murphy-O'Connor 1971a: 222). The series of warnings is much more elaborate than the promise and addresses various groups:

> all those who fail to obey the prescriptions (CD 7.9; 19.5-6a);
> those who have entered the covenant and subsequently failed to observe the requirements expected of members (CD 8.1b-2a; 19.13b-14a; 4QD[a] 3 iii 23-25);

the 'princes of Judah', a term derived from Hos. 5.10 that is apparently applied to the political rulers of the time, (CD 8.3; 19.15b-16a; 4QD^a 3 iii 25—iv 1);

the 'builders of the wall', an expression derived from Ezek. 13.10, their followers as well as everyone who fails to obey the commandments, probably all non-members (CD 8.18b-19; 19.31b-33a).

This series of warnings is interrupted by a second promise to 'the converts of Israel who turn aside from the way of the people' (CD 8.14-18a; 19.26b-31a). Manuscripts A and B correspond as far as the general structure and argument are concerned. The main differences between both manuscripts are the scriptural proof texts used and their interpretations. Manuscript A builds on Isa. 7.17, Amos 5.26-27, Amos 9.11, and Num. 24.17. Manuscript B draws on Zech. 13.7 and Ezek. 9.4. 4QD^a 3 iii 18–iv is closer to the text of manuscript A. A number of scholars have offered theories to account for the differences between both manuscripts, and we will deal with this debate in Chapter 7 below.

Rejection of Former Members who have Turned their Backs on the Community
(CD 8.21b; CD 19.33b–20.1a)
Apostate members are threatened with exclusion from the community in the period from the death of the teacher until the coming of the Messiah of Aaron and Israel. Manuscript A breaks off soon after the beginning of this passage, and we depend on manuscript B for the remainder of the Admonition as preserved in the Cairo text.

Temporary Expulsion of Disobedient Members
(CD 20.1b-8a)
Whereas the material preceding and following the present section speaks of permanent condemnation of apostates often denying them any stake in the blessings expected at the final divine visitation, CD 20.1b-8a refers to a temporary expulsion of disobedient members. This passage has more in common with disciplinary legislation found in the Laws of the Damascus Document (cf. 4QD^a 10 i 11–ii 15 par.) and the Community Rule (cf. 1QS 6.24–7.25 par.) than the rest of the Admonition. It is frequently argued, therefore, that this material constitutes a secondary interpolation in its present context. So, for example, Murphy-O'Connor who observes with reference to this passage, 'Had CD XX, 1c-8a been found as an isolated fragment it would have been presumed that it belonged to the *Rule*...' (Murphy-O'Connor 1972b: 554-55).

A Further Condemnation of Apostates
(CD 20.8b-13a)
Here we have a further warning addressed to all those who fail to observe the commandments laid down for community members and turn their back on the 'new covenant' established 'in the land of Damascus'.

A Further Warning and Promise
(CD 20.13b-22a)
This section begins with a prediction of a period of 40 years that will pass between the teacher's death and the final judgment. The final visitation of God will bring destruction to outsiders and deliverance to faithful community members.

The Fate of 'the House of Peleg'
(CD 20.22b-25a)
The beginning of this passage is damaged, which renders its precise meaning unclear. The members of a group referred to as 'the house of Peleg' will be judged each according to their merits.

Final Warning to Apostates
(CD 20.25b-27a; 4QD[b] 3.1-4)
A final warning addresses apostate former members and non-members denying them a place in 'the midst of the camp' at the final judgment. 4QD[b] 3.4 fragmentarily preserves the additional words '[those who hold] fast to the covenant' following this warning.

Final Promise to the Faithful
(CD 20.27b-34; 4QD[a] 4.7-13; 4QD[b] 3.6-7)
Manuscript B and with it the Admonition as known from the Cairo manuscripts breaks off with a final promise of salvation to the faithful who obey the law as well as the voice of the teacher. Part of this promise consists of a communal confession (CD 20.28b-30a). 4QD[a] 4 preserves the fragmentary remains of a number of additional lines that seem to continue the blessing beyond CD 20.34.

A Catalogue of Transgressions
(4QD[e] 2 i 9–ii 18; 6QD 5.1-5)
A fragmentary catalogue of transgressions is preserved in 4QD[e] and contains a list of wrongdoings in the following areas: necromancy, sexual misdemeanours, priestly dues, skin disease and flux—apparently considered as afflictions brought upon by wrongdoing (Baumgarten 1996: 146)—revealing national secrets, apostasy, and the slaughter of pregnant animals. A

number of the issues raised in this catalogue are dealt with at greater length elsewhere in the Laws. The overlap between 4QD^e 2 ii 15-19 and 6QD 5 was identified by Milik (Baumgarten 1996: 146).

A Call to Hearken Introducing an Admonitory Passage
(4QD^e 2 ii 19-21)
These lines contain a call to hearken of the kind attested repeatedly in the Admonition of the Damascus Document, cf. 4QD^a 1 a-b.5; CD 1.1 par.; 2.2 par.; 2.14 par. This call to attention is best taken as an introduction to an admonitory passage which has not been preserved (Hempel 1998: 170).

Fragmentary Passage that Provides a Link between the Admonition and the Laws
(4QD^a 5 i 1-19; 4QD^b 5 ii 1-7)
This fragmentary text uniquely combines features characteristic of the Admonition and the Laws and seems to form a kind of bridge between both parts of the document. Thus, we find in 4QD^a 5 i 15 a reference to 'the converts of Israel', a central concept in the Admonition, alongside a reference to 'the overseer' in 4QD^a 5 i 14, a communal official who is frequently mentioned in the legal part of the document but never in the Admonition (Hempel 1998: 171-74).

The Disqualification of Various Categories of Priest
(4QD^a 5 ii 1-16 ; 4QD^b 5 iii 1-8; 4QD^h 2.1-2; 4 i 5-11)
This lengthy section on the disqualification of priests begins by barring priests with imperfect pronunciation from reading the torah lest they mislead their listeners in a capital case (cf. 4QD^a 5 ii 1-3 par.). This is followed by a number of regulations disqualifying priests from the holy service and from eating sacrificial food (cf. 4QD^a 5 ii 4-14 par.). Among the latter are included priests who have been taken captive by the gentiles and apostate priests.

Skin Disease, Flux, and Childbirth
(4QD^a 6 i-iii; 4QD^d 7; 4QD^g 1 i-ii; 4QD^h 4 ii)
This material deals with the topics of skin disease, flux, and childbirth and is based on Leviticus 12–15. The bulk of this lengthy section pertains to the priestly duty of diagnosing diseased skin, heads, and beards. Further issues addressed are the treatment of men and women suffering from a discharge and the purification of women after childbirth.

On Agriculture
(4QD^a 6 iii a 2-4; iii 3b-10; iv 1-8; 4QD^b 6.2-7; 4QD^e 3 i 19-21; ii 12-21; iii 13-15; 4QD^f 2.1-5)
Two small fragments (4QD^a 6 iii a and 4QD^e 3 i) contain fragmentary remains of agricultural halakhah. 4QD^e 3 i 19 contains the faint traces of a heading written in red ink that may well constitute a heading introducing the lengthy section of laws dealing with agricultural matters (Baumgarten 1996: 147). The next preserved block of material is a substantial section dealing with the topic of gleanings and bread offerings (4QD^a 6 iii; 4QD^b 6; and 4QD^e 3 ii). The scriptural legislation on gleanings, that is portions of various crops to be left for the poor, is found in Lev. 19.9; 23.22; and Deut. 24.19-21. Like tractate *Peah* of the Mishnah the present material is concerned to clarify the maximum amount that may be gleaned, a topic not addressed in the biblical legislation. Holy bread offerings are referred to in the Bible in Num. 15.20 and Lev. 23.17. The position advanced in our text advocates an annual offering of bread, cf. 4QD^e 3 ii 20. Further agricultural halakhah is found in 4QD^a 6 iv where the topic of the fourth year produce of newly planted fruit trees is addressed, cf. Lev. 19.23-25. Finally 4QD^f 2 and 4QD^e 3 iii deal with the subject of tithing.

On Ritual Defilement and Purification
(4QD^d 8 i 3; ii 1-6; 4QD^e 3 iii 19-21; 4QD^f 2.7-13)
This section deals with two types of ritual defilement: objects and metals defiled through contact with the pagan cult and corpse impurity, and the ritual of purification to be applied in the latter case, cf. Numbers 19.

The Suspected Adulterous Wife and the Betrothed Slave Woman
(4QD^a 12.1-9; 13?; 4QD^e 4.1-21; 4QD^h 5?)
4QD^e 4.1-8 is based on Num. 5.11-31 and describes a priestly ordeal which is supposed to establish whether or not a woman accused of adultery is guilty. The remainder of this section as preserved in 4QD^e 4.9-20 par. is fragmentary but it is clear from what remains that the topic is still in the realm of relations between the sexes. 4QD^e 4.14 refers to the case of a betrothed slave woman, an issue legislated upon in Lev. 19.20-22 (Baumgarten 1996: 154).

The Jubilee Year, Transvestism, Business Ethics, and Suitable Brides
(4QD^b 7.1-7, 12-14; 4QD^d 9.1-8; 4QD^e 5.14-21; 4QD^f 3.1-15)
The theme of honesty and morality holds together the various topics addressed in this section of laws. Moreover, all of the issues raised here have a basis in scripture. The biblical legislation on the year of release on which the first topic of this passage is based is found in Leviticus 25. In particular

4QD^f 3.2-3a par. seems to refer to the redemption of property of an impoverished Israelite laid down in Lev. 25.25-28. The prohibition of transvestism found in 4QD^f 3.3b-4a is based on Deut. 22.5. The demands for ethical standards in business transactions laid down in 4QD^f 3.4b-7a are explicitly anchored in the admonition not to wrong one's neighbour laid down in Lev. 25.14. Finally, 4QD^f 3.7b-15 par. contains the remains of a lengthy section of guidelines on selecting suitable brides and repeatedly draws on Deuteronomy 22. Thus, the prohibitions of ploughing with an ox and a donkey and mixing wool and linen which are here applied to unsuitable matches are found in Deut. 22.10-11, and the issue of a groom denying his bride's virginity is based on Deut. 22.13-21. The passage ends with a reference to an examination of brides by suitable women in order to verify or falsify such claims (cf. also 4QOrdinances [4Q159 2-4]) (Tigay 1993).

An Admonition Not to Bear a Grudge
(4QD^a 7 i 1-5)
This fragmentary section is made up of two small fragments and takes up the topic of rebuke dealt with also in CD 9.2-8a, 18 and is based on Lev. 19.17-18.

A Fragmentary Section Mentioning the Camp and the Overseer
(4QD^a 7 ii 1-10; iii 1-7; 4QD^b 8.1-7)
This group of fragments preserves very little text although from the references to the overseer and the camp in 4QD^a 7 iii 3 we may infer that they comprise remains of a portion of communal legislation.

On Swearing Oaths
(CD 15.1-5a; 4QD^e 6 i 20; 4QD^f 4 i 6-7)
The beginning of this passage is damaged. The preserved material contains a series of rules on swearing oaths.

Admission into the Covenant Community
(CD 15.5b–16.6a; 4QD^a 8 i 1-9; 4QD^e 6 i 21; ii 5-10, 17-19 ; 4QD^f 4 i 10-12; ii 1-7)
This passage describes the process of admission into the community by swearing the oath of the covenant. The admission process laid down here contrasts sharply with the elaborate and complex admission process prescribed in the Community Rule (1QS 6.13b-23 par.) although a comparable procedure is described in 1QS 5.7c-9a par. Towards the end of this section occurs an explicit reference to the book of *Jubilees* (CD 16.2b-4a par.) which was clearly regarded as an authoritative work by the author of this

passage. *Jubilees* is referred to here as 'the book of the divisions of the times into their jubilees and weeks', a title remarkably similar to a phrase used in the Prologue to *Jubilees* itself. 4QD[a] 8 i provides a significant amount of additional text that has been lost at the end of CD 15 as well as providing four additional words that result in an improved reading for CD 15.15 (Baumgarten 1996: 63-64; Qimron 1992: 39; Hempel 1998: 72-76).

Oaths and Vows
(CD 16.6b–9.1; 4QD[a] 8 ii 1-9; 4QD[e] 6 ii 19-21; 4QD[f] 4 ii 7-16)
This section comprises various laws dealing with oaths and vows. CD 16.6b-9 par. deals with the binding oath and is based on Deut. 23.24. The emphasis in this law is on the overriding principle of observing the law even if this would involve disregarding an oath. CD 16.10-12 legislates on women's oath. The remainder of the section appears to deal with freewill offerings. The end of page 16 is very fragmentary, and it is impossible to be sure how far exactly the subject of freewill offerings extends beyond CD 16.17a. The subject of vows and oaths seems to end in CD 9.1 with a citation of Lev. 27.29 followed by a reference to Lev. 20.23. 4QD[a] 8 ii 8, partially paralleled by 4QD[e] 6 iii 15-16, preserves an introductory formula 'as he said' introducing the citation of Lev. 27.29 in CD 9.1. This formula was lost at the end of CD 16, the page preceding CD 9 in the Cairo text.

Reproof
(CD 9.2-8a; 4QD[a] 8 ii 10; 4QD[b] 9 i 1-3; 4QD[e] 6 iii 16–vi 1; 5QD 1.1-2)
Based on Lev. 19.17-18 and Nah. 1.2 members of the covenant are required to reprove fellow members in front of witnesses on the same day as a misdeed occurs, cf. also 4QD[a] 7 i 1-5. Both 4QD[e] 6 iii 20 and 5QD 1.1 contain fragmentary remains of some additional text not found in CD 9.6-7 (Milik in Baillet, Milik, and de Vaux 1962: 181).

A Further Law on Oaths
(CD 9.8b-10a; 4QD[b] 9 i 4-5; 4QD[e] 6 iv 1-2; 5QD 1.3-5)
The subject of oaths is taken up again in CD 9.8b par. Based on an interpretation of 1 Sam. 25.26 no one is to compel another to swear an oath in a field without judges being present.

Loss or Theft of Property
(CD 9.10b-16a; 4QD[b] 9 i 5-8; 4QD[e] 6 iv 3; 5QD 1.5)
This passage prescribes the procedure for dealing with lost or stolen property. The owners of missing or stolen property are to swear a cursing oath, and property the owners of which are unknown is to be kept by the priests. Private ownership of property is presupposed here.

Witnesses
(CD 9.16b–10.3; 4QD^a 8 iii 3; 4QD^e 6 iv 11-15)
This section lays down the number of witnesses required for two types of offence. Matters of property require two witnesses to convict an offender whereas capital cases require three witnesses. This legislation is based on a particular interpretation of Deut. 17.6 and 19.15 (Schiffman 1983a: 74-78). Witnesses are to report their testimony to the overseer on the same day, cf. Num. 30.15 (Schiffman 1983a: 90-91), and the overseer is to keep a written record of these rebukes. A recently published text from Qumran Cave 4 (4Q477) seems to constitute just such a record of rebukes compiled by the overseer (Eshel 1994; Hempel 1995; Reed 1996).

Judges of the Congregation
(CD 10.4-10a; 4QD^a 8 iii 4-9; 4QD^e 6 iv 15-19)
Ten judges shall be chosen, four from the tribes of Levi and Aaron and six from Israel. They are to be aged between 25 and 60 years old. The judges need to be learned in the principles of the covenant and 'the book of Hagi'. The enigmatic book of Hagi is mentioned only in the Laws of the Damascus Document (CD 10.6b par. 4QD^a 8 iii 5 and 4QD^e 6 iv 17; CD 13.2; and CD 14.7-8 par. 4QD^b 9 v 12) and the Rule of the Congregation (1QSa 1.7). A wisdom work from Qumran Cave 4 mentions 'a vision of Hagu' (4QSapiential Work A [4Q417] 2 i 15-16). None of these references provides any concrete information on the contents of this book. It is probably a work that has not come down to us. The passage on the judges ends with a theological explanation for the upper age limit that is influenced by *Jub.* 23.9-11.

Purification with Water
(CD 10.10b-13; 4QD^a 8 iii 9-10; 4QD^e 6 iv 20-21)
This section contains stipulations on the purification of persons or objects in water.

Sabbath Code
(CD 10.14–11.18b; 4QD^a 9 i 1-4; 4QD^b 9 ii 2-3, 8; 4QD^e 6 v 1-21; 4QD^f 5 i 1-12)
The sabbath code makes up one of the lengthiest pieces of legislation on a single subject in the Laws of the Damascus Document. Based on the commandment to observe the sabbath in Deut. 5.12 the code provides a long list of restrictions to be adhered to on the sabbath. 4QD^e 6 v 17 lacks the reference to the hired labourer found in CD 11.12 alongside male and female servants, and 4QD^e 6 v 8 lacks the prohibition of spending the sabbath in the vicinity of gentiles found in both CD 11.14-15 and 4QD^f 5 i 9.

Preserving the Purity of the Altar
(CD 11.18c-21a)
This passage forbids sending offerings to the altar by the hand of a ritually impure person as this would bring about pollution of the altar itself.

The House of Worship
(CD 11.21b–12.1a; 4QD^f 5 i 15-17)
A number of rules contain prescriptions for entering 'the house of worship'. The term 'house of worship' is a *hapax legomenon*, that is a term that occurs only here, not only in the Damascus Document but among the corpus of non-biblical scrolls as a whole. Its meaning is uncertain. It may refer to some local place of worship.

Prohibition of Sexual Relations in Jerusalem
(CD 12.1b-2a; 4QD^f 5 i 17-18)
This law requires the highest standards of ritual purity for Jerusalem and forbids any sexual relations in the city. A similar rule is found in the Temple Scroll, cf. 11QT^a 45.11-12.

Those Ruled by the Spirits of Belial
(CD 12.2b-3a; 4QD^f 5 i 18-19)
This law demands that anyone who is ruled by the spirits of Belial is to be judged like a ghost or a wizard, that is according to Lev. 20.27 subjected to the death penalty. Belial is a term frequently found in the scrolls with reference to the leader of the evil forces, cf. CD 4.12b–5.19 above.

Desecration of the Sabbaths and the Festivals
(CD 12.3b-6a; 4QD^b 9 iii 1; 4QD^f 5 i 19-21)
Anyone who desecrates the sabbaths or the festivals is not to be put to death but to be kept watch over by guardians. This is in contrast to the biblical law in Exod. 35.2 and Num. 15.35 as well as *Jub.* 50.8, 12-13 where the death penalty is prescribed for violators of the sabbath.

Relations with Gentiles
(CD 12.6b-11a; 4QD^a 9 i 16-17; 4QD^b 9 iii 1-4; 4QD^f 5 i 21; ii 2-4)
A number of restrictions on dealings with gentiles, mainly in the area of trade, are laid down here. Of interest is the prohibition of selling to the gentiles servants who have 'entered into the covenant of Abraham'.

Purity Regulations
(CD 12.11b-20a; 4QD^a 9 ii 1-7; 4QD^f 5 ii 9)
This small collection of purity regulations begins with various rules on the

preparation and consumption of various animals, defilement with oil (see Baumgarten 1967), and the defilement of items in the house with a dead person.

Announcement of Statutes for the Wise Leader
(CD 12.20b-22a; 4QD^a 9 ii 7-8)
These lines announce statutes for the wise leader, the *maskil*, and an ordinance for the seed of Israel without any statutes following these announcements. A heading remarkably similar to CD 12.20b-21a is found in the Community Rule in 1QS 9.12 followed by a series of statutes. It is likely that some material following these lines was lost from the Laws of the Damascus Document.

The Meeting of the Camps
(CD 12.22b–13.7a; 4QD^a 9 ii 14-15; 4QD^b 9 iv 1-3; 4QD^f 5 ii 20-21)
A minimum number of ten males is required to form a camp. The members of the camps are to organize themselves in tens, fifties, hundreds, and thousands. These figures are based on Israel's organization in the wilderness, cf. Exod. 18.21, 25. Every group of ten requires the presence of a priest learned in the book of Hagu. Apart from the priest a more experienced levite may exercise leadership in the camp, and in some circumstances the overseer may be required to instruct the priest. It seems unlikely that all of these authority figures mentioned here operated simultaneously in any real community. Rather, the material on the authority structure in the camp appears to have undergone development perhaps reflecting changes in the actual authority structure of a community.

The Overseer over the Camp
(CD 13.7b–14.2; 4QD^a 9 ii 18–iii 19; 4QD^b 9 iv 3–v 6)
This section describes the duties of the overseer over the camp. The figures of the priest or the levite encountered in CD 12.22b–13.7a par. are entirely absent from this lengthy passage which indicates that at some point in the development of the Laws the figure of the overseer seems to have become the dominant authority in the camp. Apart from pastoral oversight over his camp the overseer's main responsibilities concern the admission of new members and matters of trade.

The Meeting of all the Camps
(CD 14.3-18a; 4QD^a 10 i 1-11; 4QD^b 9 v 6-14; 4QD^c 2.1-2)
Whereas CD 12.22b–14.2 par. dealt with meetings of individual camps, the present passage deals with the meeting of all the camps. We are not told in this passage how frequently such meetings of all the camps took place.

However, in the context of an expulsion ceremony at the end of the Damascus Document, 4QD^a 11.16-18 refers to a meeting of the inhabitants of the camps in the third month, a gathering that may be identical to what is envisaged in the present passage. The meetings of all the camps are said to comprise priests, levites, Israelites, and proselytes all of whom are to be mustered and seated in strict order. 4QD^b 9 v 8 lacks the reference to the proselytes found in CD 14.4 but 4QD^b 9 v 10 includes this group as in CD 14.6. In analogy to the meeting of individual camps presided over by an overseer, the overseer over all the camps presides over the meetings of all the camps. Together with the judges the overseer is responsible for the collection of a charity contribution deducted from the wages of community members to be distributed to those in need. Whereas CD 14.13 describes a monthly charitable collection, there is not sufficient space in 4QD^a 10 i 6 for the words 'every month'. 4QD^a may, therefore, refer to a one-off collection.

The Penal Code
(CD 14.18b-22; 4QD^a 10 i 11–ii 15; 4QD^b 9 vi 1-5; 4QD^d 11 i 1-8; ii 1-2; 4QD^e 7 i 1-15)
Until the recent publication of the Cave 4 manuscripts of the Damascus Document, only the fragmentary beginning of a penal code was preserved at the bottom of CD 14. A substantial amount of new material containing penal legislation is now attested in four Cave 4 manuscripts. The bulk of the D penal code resembles the penal code as preserved in 1QS 6.24–7.25; 4QS^d V.1; 4QS^e I.4-15; II. 3-8; 4QS^g 3.2-4; 4a-b. 1-7; 5a-c. 1-9; 6a-e. 1-5. Of particular interest are, however, a series of offences preserved in 4QD that are absent from the penal code as long known from 1QS. The additional offences attested in 4QD^b and 4QD^e for the first time are despising the judgment of the many, taking someone's food against the law, improper marital intercourse, and murmuring against the fathers or mothers of the congregation. This last offence of murmuring against the mothers of the congregation is noteworthy because it illustrates that the Damascus Document presupposes women as part of the organizational structure of the community. Predictably, the punishment for grumbling against the fathers of the congregation is permanent exclusion whereas the same behaviour towards the mothers of the congregation results in punishment lasting ten days.

A Ritual of Expulsion and the End of the Damascus Document
(4QD^a 11.1-20; 4QD^e 7 i 15-21; ii 11-15)
Following the penal code two manuscripts from Cave 4 preserve the text of the final portion of the Damascus Document. This section includes an

admonition to accept one's judgment (4QD^a 11.1-5a par.), an expulsion ceremony (4QD^a 11.5b-14b par.), a section dealing with those who fail to isolate ostracized members (4QD^a 11.14c-16a), an annual assembly in the third month (4QD^a 11.16b-18a par.), and the conclusion of the document (4QD^a 11.18b-20 par.). The end of the document is followed by an empty handle sheet in 4QD^a and numerous empty ruled lines and an empty ruled column in 4QD^e. Fragmentary remains of the final column of the document are also preserved in 4QD^d 16 (cf. Stegemann 1998b).

Further Reading

On the catalogue of transgressions

Baumgarten, J.M.

2000   'The Laws of the Damascus Document: Between the Bible and the Mishnah', in J.M. Baumgarten, E. Chazon, and A. Pinnick (eds.), *The Damascus Document: A Centennial of Discovery. Proceedings of the Third International Symposium of the Orion Center* (STDJ, 34; Leiden: E.J. Brill): 17-26.

Hempel, C.

2000   'The Laws of the Damascus Document and 4QMMT', in J.M. Baumgarten, E. Chazon, and A. Pinnick (eds.), *The Damascus Document: A Centennial of Discovery. Proceedings of the Third International Symposium of the Orion Center* (STDJ, 34; Leiden: E.J. Brill): 69-84.

On the priestly disqualification material

Baumgarten, J.M.

1992b   'The Disqualifications of Priests in 4Q Fragments of the "Damascus Document", a Specimen of the Recovery of pre-Rabbinic Halakha', in J. Trebolle Barrera and L. Vegas Montaner (eds.), *The Madrid Qumran Congress: Proceedings of the International Congress on the Dead Sea Scrolls, Madrid 18–21 March 1991* (STDJ, 11; 2 vols.; Leiden: E.J. Brill): II, 503-13.

On the material dealing with skin disease

Baumgarten, J.M.

1990   'The 4Q Zadokite Fragments on Skin Disease', *JJS* 41: 153-65.

Qimron, E.

1991   'Notes on the 4Q Zadokite Fragments on Skin Disease', *JJS* 42: 256-59.

On the agricultural halakhah

Baumgarten, J.M.

1987   'The Laws of ^cOrlah and First Fruits in the Light of Jubilees, the Qumran Writings, and Targum Ps. Jonathan', *JJS* 38: 195-202.

1995   'A Qumran Text with Agrarian Halakhah', *JQR* 86: 1-8.

Since the latter article appeared the numbering of the fragments has changed. The numbering used in this book follows Baumgarten's *editio princeps* of the 4QD manuscripts.

On the sabbath code

Schiffman, L.H.
  1975   *The Halakha at Qumran* (SJLA, 16; Leiden: E.J. Brill): 77-133.

On the penal code

Baumgarten, J.M.
  1992d   'The Cave 4 Versions of the Qumran Penal Code', *JJS* 43: 268-76.
Hempel, C.
  1997   'The Penal Code Reconsidered', in M.J. Bernstein, F. García Martínez, and
            J. Kampen (eds.), *Legal Texts and Legal Issues: Proceedings of the Second Meet-
            ing of the International Organization for Qumran Studies, Published in Honour
            of Joseph M. Baumgarten* (STDJ, 23; Leiden: E.J. Brill): 337-48.

On the material reconstruction of the 4QD fragments

Stegemann, H.
  2000   'Towards Physical Reconstructions of the Qumran Damascus Document
            Scrolls', in J.M. Baumgarten, E. Chazon and A. Pinnick (eds.), *The Dam-
            ascus Document: A Centennial of Discovery. Proceedings of the Third Interna-
            tional Symposium of the Orion Center* (STDJ, 34; Leiden: E.J. Brill): 177-200.

4

THE COMPOSITE CHARACTER OF THE DAMASCUS DOCUMENT

1. The Admonition

A great deal of scholarly attention has been devoted to attempts at outlining the literary growth of the Admonition of the Damascus Document. It needs to be borne in mind, however, that all the analyses of the Admonition to be presented below go back to the time prior to the publication of the Cave 4 manuscripts of the Damascus Document. Most scholars regard the Admonition as a composite work, and a variety of proposals have been made on the compositional make-up of this part of the document. Some have not been convinced by the results of this source-critical work on D (Dimant 1984: 485-87; van der Woude 1992: 49-56). Furthermore, Knibb (1994) has expressed doubts as to whether it is possible to isolate a pre-Teacher stage in the growth of the Admonition.

A variety of hypotheses have emerged from those who have attempted to offer an analysis of the literary growth of the Admonition of the Damascus Document.

I. Rabinowitz perceives three types of material in the Damascus Document (1954: 13-14 n. 8):

1. An Admonition written in verse (CD 1.1–3.20; 5.13-17; 8.3-9 [=19.16-21]; 20.32-33);
2. Comments and glosses written in prose (CD 3.21–5.12; 5.18–8.2; 8.9-19 [=19.22-33]; 19.34–20.31; 20.34).
3. Halakhic material (CD 9–16).

Along similar lines, R.A. Soloff, taking up a suggestion by Morton Smith and reporting the results of a group of students from Drews University Graduate School, argues in favour of distinguishing in the Admonition of

CD a series of prophecies written in verse from prose interpolations (Soloff 1958).

O. Schwarz, in the course of a study that is primarily concerned with the relationship of the Admonition to the Old Testament identifies three types of material in the Admonition (1965):

1. Narrative texts (CD 1.1-13a; 2.2a-13d; 2.14a–3.20d; and 4.4d-12b).
2. Exegetical texts:
    i.   passages that provide scriptural backing for material elaborated in sections A or C (*Schriftbezug*) (CD 1.13b–2.1d; 3.20e–4.2b; 4.12c-14d; 5.13b–6.4b; 7.8c-14a; 7.21b–8.3a; 8.9b-10a, 14a-18a, 20-21a;19.1d-2b, 5-9b, 15b-16b, 21d-22c, 26d-31a; 20.16b-17a).
    ii. passages that interpret scripture in the light of the history of the community (*Damaskuspescher*) (CD 4.2c-4c, 14e-19a; 6.4c-11b; 7.14b-21a; 8.10b-12a = 19.22d-24c; 19.9c-13b).
3. Legal texts:
    i.   legal texts that reflect a positive attitude to the biblical legal tradition (CD 4.19b–5.13a; 6.11c–7.6a par. 19; 7.6b-9a par. 19; 8.3b-9a par. 19; 8.12b-13a par. 19; 8.18b-19e par. 19).
    ii. legal texts whose relation to the Bible is restricted to the use of biblical language and ideas (CD 19.33d–20.34).

Moreover, Schwarz argues that the exegetical material presupposes the narrative and legal material.

In the same year as Schwarz's dissertation appeared, A.-M. Denis (1965) argued that CD may be divided into four parts:

1. CD 1.1–4.6a comprises three admonitions, displays many terminological similarities to Daniel and dates from around the same period, that is around 164 BCE. This part of CD reflects a movement rather than an organized community.
2. CD 4.6b–7.4 reflects a much more tightly organized community whose opposition towards other Jews has hardened.
3. CD 7.4–8.21 par. CD 19.1-33a and CD 19.33b–20.34 is less homogenous and may be subdivided into four pericopes:
    i.   CD 7.4-13 par. 19.1-7.
    ii. CD 7.13–8.13 par. 19.7-26.
    iii. CD 8.14-21 par. 19.26-34 and 19.35–20.15.
    iv. CD 20.15-34.
    The first and third pericopes reflect the community behind CD in its most developed form and employ the self-designation 'perfect

holy ones'. The second pericope goes back to the same period as the first part of the document (i.e. CD 1.1–4.6a). The fourth pericope falls into two components. CD 20.15-27 represents an intermediary stage in the development of the community between the second and third pericopes. CD 20.27-34 displays notable terminological links with the Community Rule (1QS) but the community that emerges is not yet as highly developed as in the first and third pericopes and 1QS.

D. CD 9–16 comprising the Law Code.

In a monograph two years later, Denis's results differ from the above by grouping together the Law Code in CD 9–16 and the 'Petite Code' in CD 6.12–7.4a. Thus, in his monograph (1967) Denis's second document comprises CD 4.6b–6.11.

In a series of articles that appeared in *Revue biblique* between 1970 and 1972, Jerome Murphy-O'Connor offers a source-critical analysis of the Admonition (1970, 1971a, 1972a, 1972b). He distinguishes the following literary components:

1. *An Essene missionary document* (CD 2.14–6.1) composed in order to win Palestinian converts to their movement by a group of exiles returning from Babylon to Palestine in the Maccabean period. This document was later adapted to a different purpose with the addition of the historical and theological introductions in CD 1.1–2.13.

2. *A memorandum* (CD 6.11b–8.3) designed to encourage recent converts to the movement to persevere with the demands placed upon them in the face of hostility and the threat of assimilation posed by the outside world. This memorandum comprises a summary of the duties of community members spelt out more fully in the legal part of the document and displays strong links to the Holiness Code.

3. *A document comprising a critique of 'the Princes of Judah'* (CD 8.3-18) condemning the ruling class of Judah for its lack of support of the Essene movement. This document was written in the first half of the second century BCE by the teacher of righteousness or one of his followers. In its present context as part of the Admonition it has been adapted to its new function of addressing community members whose loyalty to the cause was waning.

4. *The Grundschrift (original core) of CD 19.33–20.22b* (i.e. CD 19.33b–20.1b; 20.8b-13, 17b-22b). This *Grundschrift* was written after the death of the teacher of righteousness (cf. CD 19.35–20.1) with the intention of winning back the growing number of disaffected community members.

5. *A fragment of community legislation* (CD 20.1c-8a).

6. *A Pesher on Num. 21.18* (CD 6.2-11a), the Well Midrash, a self-contained unit that serves to provide a transition between the missionary document and the memorandum.
7. *Historical and theological introductions* (CD 1.1–2.13) were added in order to adapt the missionary document to a new situation when it had become necessary to reinforce the commitment of disaffected community members.
8. *The conclusion to the Admonition* (CD 20.22c-34) which goes back to the compiler of the Admonition.

Apart from these literary components Murphy-O'Connor further argues for the presence of three types of interpolation:

i. *Interpolations enforcing the hortatory character of the Admonition* going back to the compiler of the Admonition (CD 3.15b-16a; 6.10b; 8.19; 19.10a; 20.13c-17a).
ii. *Interpolations reflecting hostility between the community and an individual* which also go back to the compiler of the Admonition and allude to the source of the troubles his community is facing (CD 4.19; 8.13).
iii. *Miscellaneous glosses* (CD 1.13b, c, 20d-21a; 3.8a, 17b-18a; 5.2b-6a, 18-19; 7.6b-8; 7.13c–8.1a).

In a monograph on the Admonition P.R. Davies (1983) distinguishes three stages in the literary development of the document as represented by the mediaeval manuscripts:

1. *The original document* comprises CD 1.1–7.9 (pp. 195, 198 although elsewhere he seems to regard the brief warning in CD 7.9-10a as part of the original document, cf. pp. 105, 143) and the original nucleus of CD 20.27b-34 (pp. 194-97) plus the Laws (CD 9–16). The coherently structured original form of the Damascus Document goes back to the time before the emergence of the Qumran community. It can be subdivided into:
   i. an historical part comprising three discourses (CD 1.1–4.12a);
   ii. a legal part (CD 4.12b–7.9 [10a?]) made up of a variety sources:
      a. a midrash on Isa. 24.17 in CD 4.12b-19;
      b. an originally independent list of accusations now presented as interpreting the midrash in CD 4.20–5.16;
      c. an originally independent composition explaining the origin of the community's laws in CD 5.17–6.11a;
      d. a summary of the community's laws in CD 6.11b–7.4a followed by
      e. a promise and brief warning in CD 7.4b-6a, 9-10a.

The community behind the original document later gave rise to the Qumran community. The former's ideology is rooted in the priestly exilic literature such as the Holiness Code and Ezekiel. The original Damascus Document goes back to the same circles as lie behind the Book of *Jubilees* and parts of *1 Enoch*.

2. *Two passages comprising 'Warnings'* (CD 7.10b–8.2; 8.2-19) were added to the original document expanding the brief, original warning in CD 7.9-10a. These additional warnings are characterized and were inspired by tensions between the community and external authorities.

3. A *Qumranic redaction* comprising CD 19.33b–20.27a as well as numerous secondary additions. The community reflected in this material is characterized by its adherence to a teacher and referred to itself as 'the *new* covenant in the land of Damascus' (CD 19.33-34, cf. also CD 20.12). Key concerns reflected in this material are the defection of community members and the death of the teacher. Within the lengthy Qumranic redaction, CD 20.1b-8a is identified as a secondary insertion addressing rebellious community members. Davies allows for the possibility that the Qumranic redaction of the document originated successively (p. 199). He further isolates four categories of secondary glosses associated with the Qumranic redaction of CD (their exact distribution is marked with brackets of the type < > in the translation appended to Davies's monograph [pp. 233-67]):

    i. references to an individual opponent of the Qumran community (CD 1.14-18; 4.19-20; 8.12-13);

    ii. rewriting of community history from a Qumranic perspective in CD 1.1–2.1 including the secondary insertion of the reference to the teacher of righteousness in CD 1.11;

    iii. reapplication of warnings composed against outsiders to address members of the Qumran community in CD 8.2-19;

    iv. 'least certain' (p. 198) additions reflecting a hostile attitude to the Temple (CD 1.3 [erroneously listed as 1.4 on p. 201]; 6.12b-14a, 18b-19).

In an unpublished doctoral dissertation Mark Boyce (1988) offers a detailed analysis of the composite character of the Admonition of the Damascus Document. Some of his results appeared in an article in 1990. Boyce distinguishes three strands of material in the Admonition which he labels poetical, redactional, and midrashic. He dates the poetry to the lifetime of the Teacher (140–110 BCE), the redactional material somewhat later (88–70 BCE), and the midrashic sections soon thereafter, since the earliest manuscript from Cave 4 containing these sections goes back to the second half of the first century.

Boyce's results may be summed up as follows:

1. Poetical sections (CD 1.1–3.20 [excluding various redactional additions]; 5.11–6.3; 6.11–7.10 [excluding a secondary addition in 7.6-9a]; 8.1-9 = 19.13-21; 20.27-34).
2. Redactional material (CD 1.5-6, 10, 12-14; 2.9; 3.15-16; 4.6–5.11; 7.10-13; 7.22–8.3; 19.7-13; 8.12-21 = 19.24-33; 19.33–20.27). Within the redactional material Boyce differentiates between a number of sources used by the redactor (CD 4.12-19; 20.22-25, 25-27) and material composed by the redactor.
3. Midrashic material (CD 3.20–4.6; 6.3-11; 7.14-21; 8.9-12 = 19.21-24).
4. Boyce further singles out a number of secondary additions and glosses interspersed throughout the Admonition:
    i. 'Anti-Temple material' (CD 1.3; 6.12-14);
    ii. 'the New Covenant' (CD 6.18-19; 20.12);
    iii. 'the "Messianic" references' (CD 2.12; 5.21–6.1);
    iv. 'Glosses' (CD 1.16; 5.15; 6.15).

In contrast to P.R. Davies, M. Boyce maintains on the basis of his analysis of the poetry of CD that the references to the teacher of righteousness in CD 1.11 and CD 20.27-34 form an integral part of both sections and should not be regarded as secondary Qumranic additions.

Finally, most recently I have proposed, with reference to the accounts of community origins in the Admonition, to differentiate between those accounts that describe the emergence of the movement as a single event (CD 1.3-9a; 2.8b-9a, 11-13; 3.12b-17a) and more complex descriptions that describe community origins in several stages (CD 1.9b-11a; 3.10c–4.4a; 5.20–6.11a) (Hempel 1999). I have further argued that the former go back to the parent movement of the teacher community whereas as the latter go back to the followers of the teacher.

2. The Laws

The source-critical studies of the Admonition dealt with above tend to refer to the Laws of the Damascus Document only briefly, often treating them as a single building block in the growth of the document. A number of scholars have, however, acknowledged the composite nature of that collection, some of them very early in the history of the study of the document. Thus, already in his *editio princeps* in 1910 Schechter observes with reference to CD and the Laws in particular that one gains the impression that we are dealing with extracts from a larger work, put together, however, in a haphazard way, with little regard to completeness or order. This is particularly discernible in the legal part. (1910: x)

Schechter's impression was probably partly, though perhaps not entirely, based on his original ordering of pages CD 15–16 which was later corrected by Milik on the basis of the Cave 4 manuscripts (for details see Chapter 2 above). Similarly Denis notes with regard to the Laws in CD 9–16, 'Commes tous les codes, il contient des éléments de plusieurs époques' (1965: 32). More recently, L.H. Schiffman and J.M. Baumgarten have expressed the view that the Laws of D are composite (Schiffman 1983a: 9; Baumgarten 1992e: 57).

An important article by A. Rubinstein (1952) constitutes a notable exception. Rubinstein offers a source-critical analysis of the Laws of the Damascus Document and distinguishes five components:

1. *CD 9.1–10.10.* This section poses considerable problems to Rubinstein since he too was writing before the reversal of the order of CD 15–16. He observes that it is out of place in its present context.
2. *CD 10.10–12.18. Urban halakhah* characterized by the occurrence of so-called 'urbanisms' such as 'city' and 'house'.
3. *CD 12.19-23. Epitome* which originated either as the conclusion to the urban halakhah or was composed by an editor in order to form a bridge between the camp rules and the urban halakhah.
4. *CD 13.1–16.5. Camp rules* which resemble the Community Rule.
5. *CD 16.6-15. General halakhah* which constitutes a later addition and displays affinities to CD 9.1–10.10 and is similarly out of place.

On the basis of these source-critical observations Rubinstein proposes the development of the document as a whole in three stages:

i. *CD 1–8. The Admonition* without CD 7.6-8.
ii. *CD 7.6-8 and CD 13.1–16.5. Camp rules.*
iii. *CD 10.10–12.18. Urban halakhah.*

The key criterion employed by Rubinstein for distinguishing the two main components of the Laws, urban halakhah and camp rules, are what he calls 'urbanisms' which characterize the 'urban halakhah'. His division of the Laws into urban halakhah and camp rules—and with it a basic acceptance of the headings and dividers given in the document itself (cf. CD 12.19; 12.22-23)—has been very influential, cf. the recent translation by E. Cook in which a division is advocated between 'camp rules' and 'city rules' (Wise, Abegg, and Cook 1996: 50). I have expressed doubts regarding the value of the so-called 'urbanisms' as a source-critical criterion since they are frequently derived from scripture rather than necessarily reflecting the lifestyle of the author's group (Hempel 1998: 11-12).

Furthermore, two studies by students of John Strugnell at Harvard have dealt with the literary growth of the Laws. Unlike previous scholars these studies incorporate the evidence of the Cave 4 manuscripts in the broadest of terms, presumably on the basis of Milik's outline (1959: 51-52). In an unpublished paper P. Tiller divides the Laws into four main parts (Tiller 1987):

1. *Legal code* (4Q material preceding the CD Laws, CD 15–12.22);
2. *Community rules* (CD 12.22–14.19);
3. *The penal code* (CD 14.20-22; 4QD) curiously distinguished from the community rules;
4. *Liturgy for the Feast of the Renewal of the Covenant* (4QD).

In an unpublished dissertation Davis (1992) distinguishes four stages in the compositional development of the Laws:

1. *A pre-Qumranic legal code* (4QD[a] skin disease material; 6Q15; CD 15.1-5; 16.6-9, 10; 9.10-16; 10.10–12.20);
2-3. *Sectarian rules that apply to communities outside of Qumran* (CD 10.4-10; 12.22–13.7; 14.3-10, 12-15 and the end of D as attested in 4QD[a]);
4. *A Qumranic redaction* (CD 15.5–16.6; 9.16–10.3; 12.20-22; 13.5-20; 13.22–14.2; and 14.10-12).

Most recently I have offered a source- and redaction-critical analysis of the Laws (Hempel 1998). I was able to include the recently published Cave 4 manuscripts comprehensively for the first time and distinguish four blocks of material:

1. *A stratum of halakhah* which may be subdivided into:
   i.   halakhic exposition of Scripture in the Laws of CD par. 4QD (CD 16.6b-17a, 17b-20?; 9.1par.-10a; 10.14–11.21a);
   ii. halakhic exposition lacking an explicit reference to Scripture (CD 10.10b-13; 12.6b-11a);
   iii. halakhah in the additional legal material in 4QD (4QD[a] 5 ii par.; 6 i-iv par.; 4QD[e] 3 i; 4QD[f] 2 par.; 4QD[d] 8 i-ii par.; 4QD[e] 4 par.; 4QD[f] 3 par.).

This stratum does not presuppose a particular community within Israel but has a national orientation. It is, moreover, firmly rooted in Scripture and displays a considerable degree of formal cohesion. Those parts of the Laws that form part of the halakhah stratum show few signs of redactional activity and updating in contrast to the communal legislation.

2. *A stratum of community organization* (CD 15.5b-6a; 15.7b–16.2a par.; 9.10b-16a par.; 9.19b–10.7a par.; 12.22b-23a; 13.1b-7a, b, 12b-13, 15b-16a, 20 par.; 14.3-6b, 8b-12a, 12c-22; 4QDᵃ 10 i-ii par.) containing prescriptions for the organization of a particular community within Israel. This stratum has undergone extensive redactional reworking.

3. *Miscellaneous halakhah* (CD 11.21b–12.2a par.; 12.11b-18).

4. *Miscellaneous traditions and redactional passages*:

   i. remnants of traditions dealing with the *maskil* that have become merged with the material on the overseer (CD 12.20b-22a; 13.7c-8, 14-15a, 22 par.);

   ii. passages promoting concerns reminiscent of the book of *Jubilees* (CD 16.2b-6a; 10.7b-10a par.; 12.2b-6a);

   iii. a Serekh redaction, that is a redaction intended to bring the communal legislation into line with the Community Rule (the references to 'the many' in CD 15.8 and 4QDᵃ 10 ii 7; 11.1. Further, CD 13.11-12a; 14.6c-8a, 12b par.; 4QDᵉ 7 i 11a; 4QDᵃ 11.7b-8a);

   iv. a Damascus redaction, that is a redaction intended to present the whole of the Damascus Document as a unified composition (4QDᵃ 5 i par.; the reference to the time of wickedness in 4QDᶠ 2.12 par.; CD 15.6b-7a; 12.19-20a; 12.23b–13.1a; 13.23–14.2a; 14.19 par.);

   v. a catalogue of transgressions (4QDᵉ 2 i 9–ii 21). The main body of the catalogue lists a number of issues that are dealt with at greater length elsewhere in the Laws. I have considered the possibility that it originated independently. Elsewhere I offer a discussion of the potential significance of this catalogue for the growth of the Laws (Hempel in Baumgarten, Chazon, and Pinnick 2000).

   vi. an expulsion ceremony and the end of the Damascus Document (4QDᵃ 11 par.) This text makes use of traditions such as the covenant renewal ceremony as well as displaying significant terminological links to the Admonition. It appears to be poorly edited and to go back to a late stage in the formation of the document.

   vii. miscellaneous statements, mostly fragmentary, which have not been assigned to any of the larger components (CD 15.1-5a; 13.9-10, 16b-19; 14.2b).

Just as the source-critical studies of the Admonition dealt with the Laws only fleetingly so the analyses of the Laws discussed above incorporate the

Admonition only cursorily. By way of concluding the part of this volume that is devoted to the Damascus Document in Chapter 8 below I will sketch some avenues for arriving at a synthesis which takes the evidence of the whole document into account more fully than has been the case thus far.

Further Reading

On the composite character of the Admonition

Boyce, M.
    1988   'The Poetry of the Damascus Document' (University of Edinburgh: PhD thesis).

Davies, P.R.
    1983   *The Damascus Covenant: An Interpretation of the 'Damascus Document'* (JSOTSup, 25; Sheffield: Sheffield Academic Press).

Denis, A.-M.
    1965   'Évolution de structures dans la secte de Qumrân', in J. Giblet *et al.* (eds.), *Aux origines de l'église* (RechBib, 7; Louvain: Desclée de Brouwer): 23-49.
    1967   *Les thèmes de connaissance dans le Document de Damas* (Louvain: Publications Universitaires).

Hempel, C.
    1999   'Community Origins in the Damascus Document in the Light of Recent Scholarship', in D.W. Parry and E. Ulrich (eds.), *The Provo International Conference on the Dead Sea Scrolls: Technological Innovations, New Texts, and Reformulated Issues* (STDJ, 30; Leiden: E.J. Brill): 316-29.

Murphy-O'Connor, J.
    1970   'An Essene Missionary Document? CD II, 14-VI, 1', *RB* 77: 201-29.
    1971a   'A Literary Analysis of Damascus Document VI, 2-VIII, 3', *RB* 78: 210-31.
    1972a   'The Critique of the Princes of Judah (CD VIII, 3-19)', *RB* 79: 200-16.
    1972b   'A Literary Analysis of Damascus Document XIX, 33-XX, 34', *RB* 79: 544-64.

Rabinowitz, I.
    1954   'A Reconsideration of "Damascus" and "390 Years" in the "Damascus" ("Zadokite") Fragments', *JBL* 73: 11-35.

Schwarz, O.J.R.
    1965   *Der erste Teil der Damaskusschrift und das Alte Testament* (Diest: Lichtland).

Soloff, R.A.
    1958   'Towards Uncovering Original Texts in the Zadokite Documents', *NTS* 5: 62-67.

On the composite character of the Laws

Davis, R.
    1992   'The History of the Composition of the Damascus Document Statutes (CD 9-16 + 4QD)' (University of Harvard: PhD dissertation).

Hempel, C.
    1998   *The Laws of the Damascus Document: Sources, Traditions and Redaction* (STDJ, 29; Leiden: E.J. Brill).

Rubinstein, A.
    1952   'Urban Halakhah and Camp Rules in the "Cairo Fragments of a Damascene Covenant"', *Sefarad* 12: 283-96.

5

THE DAMASCUS DOCUMENT AND THE QUEST FOR THE ORIGINS AND EARLY HISTORY OF THE 'QUMRAN COMMUNITY'

The descriptions of the origin and history of a movement repeatedly attested in the Admonition of the Damascus Document have generated a great deal of interest. Scholars have attempted to use these accounts—often in conjunction with veiled references to communal history in other works—to reconstruct the history of the 'Qumran community'. I have placed the latter expression in inverted commas because, as will become clear shortly, I am convinced along with a number of scholars that the scrolls reflect more than one community, and that only one of the communities reflected in the scrolls lived at the Qumran site. I will divide what follows into three parts dealing respectively with the overall identification of the community described in the Admonition, their place of origin, and their history. As far as possible I will deal with all of these questions first and foremost on the basis of the evidence of the Damascus Document.

1. The Identification of the Community(ies)

The particular question of the overall identification of the community(ies) behind the Damascus Document is one that is today inevitably informed by one's evaluation of the entire library. This was not the case in the earliest phase of research on the Damascus Document which was conducted prior to the discoveries at Qumran. In the pre-Qumran phase of Damascus Document research a number of different identifications were proposed. S. Schechter argued that the group behind the document were Zadokites, hence the title for his edition (*Fragments of a Zadokite Work*), and that the object of their polemic were the Pharisees (1910: xvi-xxi). The French scholar I. Lévi concurred with Schechter that the sect's opponents were the Pharisees, and proposed an identification of the sect as Sadducees (1911: 165, 168-70). We note in passing here that a Sadducean identification of the group behind the scrolls has recently been revived by Lawrence Schiffman (1990) on the basis of his interpretation of 4QMMT. L. Ginzberg (1976) referred to the group responsible for CD as 'an unknown Jewish sect' that emerged in Palestine towards the end of the second century BCE from among the Pharisees. C. Rabin (1957) also argued for a Pharisaic background of the group behind CD. R.H. Charles (1977) preferred to distinguish the group behind CD from the Sadducees at large by speaking of 'reformed Sadducees'. A number of scholars proposed identifications of the group reflected in CD that range from the early Christian period to the Middle Ages. These identifications have not commanded much support, and the palaeographical date of the oldest Cave 4 manuscript (4QD^a [4Q266]) around the first half of the first-century BCE as well as the recent radiocarbon dating of another of the Cave 4 manuscripts (4QD^b [4Q267]) to the second century BCE are impossible to reconcile with such hypotheses. The great majority of scholars favour, however, an identification of the community behind the Damascus Document with the ancient Jewish group of the Essenes as described in the writings of the first-century Jewish historian Josephus, Philo of Alexandria, and Pliny the Elder. The Essene identification was first proposed by the Israeli scholar E.L. Sukenik (1948: 16) and spelt out at greater length in a monograph by A. Dupont-Sommer (1961). More recently G. Vermes and M. Goodman (1989) have produced a most useful book that conveniently gathers together the relevant classical texts in their original languages accompanied by Goodman's translations as well as a substantial introduction by Vermes dealing with the relationship between the Essenes and Qumran. Furthermore, T.S. Beall (1988) has offered a detailed analysis of Josephus' descriptions and the evidence of the scrolls. Among those who advocate an Essene identification some distinguish a wider Essene movement and the Qumran community (García Martínez 1988; García Martínez in García Martínez and Trebolle Barrera 1995: 77-96). Moreover, a number of scholars have argued that both groups have left their mark on the Damascus Document (Davies 1983; Hempel 1998, 1999; Knibb 1994; Murphy-O'Connor 1974, 1985). H. Stegemann's position is unusual in that he advocates understanding the Essenes as the largest group of conservative Jews at the time (Stegemann 1998a: 139-210).

Something of a methodological problem arises from reading the primary texts, that is the Dead Sea Scrolls themselves, in the light of the overall framework established by external sources, particularly Josephus's description of the Essenes. It is, of course, entirely legitimate to draw on external sources such as the classical authors, but such an undertaking should not prevent us from analysing the primary evidence in its own right first without being led by a frame of reference derived from the study of external evidence. Taking things one step further M. Goodman (1995) has recently maintained that we should allow for the possibility that the group behind the Dead Sea Scrolls is not referred to outside of its own writings and should not necessarily be identified with one of the few known groups alluded to in our sources.

2. Place of Origin

The interpretation of the Damascus Document has been at the centre of scholarly debates on the place of origin of the Essenes and the Qumran community. In essence, scholars fall into two main camps arguing either for Palestinian or Babylonian origins. The former opinion manifests itself in a variety of forms.

2.1. Palestinian Origins
2.1.1. The Ḥasidim
In a number of very influential studies a series of scholars have argued that the origins of the Essenes are to be found in the ranks of a group of pious reformers known from the Books of Maccabees as the *ḥasidim* or pious ones (Cross 1995; Hengel 1981; Milik 1959; Stegemann 1971; Vermes 1994). Others have warned against building too much on the scant evidence available on the *ḥasidim* in our sources (Davies 1977, reprinted in 1996: 5-21; Stemberger 1995: 97-102). This debate goes far beyond the confines of this book since the *ḥasidim* have been seen to lie behind large sections of the Hebrew Bible as well as at the roots of the Pharisees. W.F. Albright and C.S. Mann (1969) offer a reconstruction of community origins that constitutes a hybrid of exilic Babylonian origins and the Palestinian *ḥasidim* theory.

2.1.2. A Palestinian reform movement also reflected in *1 Enoch* and *Jubilees*
On this view the roots of the Essenes and the Qumran community are found in a reform movement of pious Jews in the third and second centuries BCE that lies behind writings such as *1 Enoch* and the book of *Jubilees* (Knibb 1989; Nickelsburg 1986; Stone 1991). D. Dimant and I have developed this theory further—Dimant by proposing that parts of *1 Enoch* may be seen as 'an early sectarian work' and I by arguing that we can isolate parts of the Admonition that go back to the reform movement behind *Jubilees* and *1 Enoch* (Dimant 1984: 544; Hempel 1999). Although

a proponent of Babylonian origins, Davies has offered a further analysis of the relationship of D to *Jubilees* and *1 Enoch* (Davies 1987: 107-34).

2.1.3. The Palestinian apocalyptic tradition

F. García Martínez prefers to speak of the forerunners of the Essene movement as the Palestinian apocalyptic tradition (García Martínez 1988). Given the scholarly debate generated by the question of defining 'apocalyptic', this choice of terminology is perhaps somewhat unfortunate.

There is, in practice, not a great deal to choose between these three positions except the preferred terminology. Each group of proponents would associate many of the same texts with their preferred choice of terminology.

2.2. Babylonian Origins

J. Murphy-O'Connor (1974) is the most prominent proponent of the theory of Babylonian origins. His theory has received support from some (Weinert 1977; Davies 1990). Others, however, have taken issue with Murphy-O'Connor's arguments and have defended the hypothesis of Palestinian origins (Charlesworth 1980; Knibb 1983; Vermes 1981).

The views for and against Babylonian origins of the group behind D are firmly rooted in the exegesis of key passages in the Admonition. The scholarly debate focuses on three not entirely unrelated hotspots, which I will deal with in turn.

2.2.1. Exilic origins—the literal versus the theological interpretation

One aspect of Murphy-O'Connor's interpretation of the Damascus Document as reflecting a movement that originated in the Babylonian exile are a number of allusions to the exile in the accounts of communal origins. In Murphy-O'Connor's view these references to the exile are best taken literally as pointing towards the community's roots in the Babylonian captivity (1970; see also Davies 1983: 122-23). This interpretation has been challenged by Knibb who argues for the presence of a theological idea, common in the literature from the late biblical and intertestamental period and reflected also in D, that the exile did not come to an end until the events of a much later age, in particular the rise of a pious reform movement in the second century BCE (1976, 1983). Finally, J.J. Collins has expressed his support for Knibb's position on this issue (1989: 170-72).

2.2.2. Šby Israel

Scholars further disagree on how to translate the first word in the phrase 'the penitents/or: returnees/or: captivity of Israel (*šby Israel*) who departed from the land of Judah to sojourn in the land of Damascus' (CD 6.5 par. 4QD[b] 2.11, cf. also CD 4.2-3; 8.16 par. 19.29), and this disagreement is closely related to the debate on Babylonian origins. The translation 'the penitents of Israel' or an equivalent is favoured by García Martínez (1994), Ginzberg (1976), Knibb (1987), Rabin (1954), Vermes (1997), as well as in the revised view of Murphy-O'Connor (1985). In favour of this view scholars have drawn attention to the occurrence of the related expression 'those who turn from sin' in CD 2.5 par. 4QD^a 2 ii 5 and CD 20.17. 'Returnees' is the preferred translation of S. Iwry (1969) and Murphy-O'Connor in his earlier work (1974). Yet a third group of scholars propose to translate the disputed phrase with 'the captivity of Israel' (Davies 1983: 241, 247, 255, 261; Rabinowitz 1954; Schechter 1910). Rabinowitz's position is slightly unusual since he takes CD 6.5 as a reference to the history of Israel rather than the history of the community behind the Damascus Document (1954: 16-17 n. 20). Finally, in the translation by Wise, Abegg, and Cook *šby Israel* is rendered 'the captives of Israel' (1996).

In the Cave 4 manuscripts the expression *šby Israel* occurs twice. In 4QD^b 2.11 it parallels CD 6.5. The second occurrence in 4QD^a 5 i 15 is not paralleled in the mediaeval manuscripts. The context in which this reference occurs is a fragmentary passage that uniquely combines terminology characteristic of the Admonition and the Laws (Hempel 1998: 171-74).

On Murphy-O'Connor's analysis of the Admonition, the statement 'the returnees of Israel who departed from the land of Judah to sojourn in the land of Damascus' describes a group of Babylonian exiles who returned to Palestine in the wake of the Maccabean victories. On this view the reference to Damascus is understood as a symbol for Babylon which brings us to the second, related exegetical issue to be dealt with in this context.

2.2.3. Damascus
Another crux in the interpretation of the Damascus Document and a linchpin of the Babylonian hypothesis is one's evaluation of the references to 'Damascus' and 'the land of Damascus' in the Damascus Document.

The Admonition of the Damascus Document includes seven references to 'Damascus' in CD 6.5, 19; 7.15, 19; 8.21 par. 19.34; 20.12, and S. Iwry has appropriately described the references to Damascus in the Admonition as something of a *Leitmotif* (Iwry 1969: 82). It is this *Leitmotif*, of course, that gave the document its now conventional name. In the Cave 4 manuscripts 'Damascus' occurs only once in 4QD^a 3 iii 20 where it parallels CD 7.19. It is noteworthy, therefore, that the term never occurs in the legal part of the document, which makes up around two thirds of the work. References to 'Damascus' are further entirely absent from the non-biblical Qumran corpus outside of D. The term is not even attested in the text until recently known as 'Serekh Damascus' (4Q265) to be dealt with in the second part of this volume. Finally, even within the Admonition itself Damascus terminology is confined to the last three pages of manuscript A (CD 6–8) and manuscript B (CD 19–20) and is entirely absent from CD 1–5.

In the scholarly literature the term is sometimes *taken literally to refer to the city and its environs in Syria* (Charles 1977: II, 792-93; Fitzmyer 1970: 16; Ginzberg 1976: 260-67; Iwry 1969: 88; Lévi 1912: 1-5; Milik 1959: 87-93; Schechter 1910: xiii; Stegemann 1998a: 149; Strickert 1986: 334). Especially since the discovery of the scrolls, most scholars now tend to understand the term as having symbolic significance. Some argue that the term *symbolically refers to Qumran* (Cross 1995: 71-73 n. 5; Knibb 1979; North 1955). Others understand Damascus as a *symbol for the Judean desert* (Stegemann 1971: 240-41) whereas a third group propose to understand the term as *referring to Babylon* (Davies 1983: 122-23; Murphy-O'Connor 1974; Rabinowitz 1954). North distinguishes the references to 'the land of Damascus' from those to '(the city of) Damascus' and argues that the former refer to the Nabataean kingdom which may well have comprised the Qumran vicinity from 87 BCE–103 CE (1955). P.R. Davies has further proposed that the references to the *new* covenant in the land of Damascus in CD 6.19; 8.21 par. 19.33-34; 20.12 go back to a Qumranic recension of the original Damascus Document (Davies 1983: 173-97). A fifth position is taken by A. Jaubert and O. Schwarz who hold that the references to Damascus allude to *Babylon as well as to Qumran* (Jaubert 1958; Schwarz 1965: 124).

The passage that lies at the heart of one's understanding of the Damascus symbolism in the Damascus Document is CD 7.14-18 where Amos 5.26-27 is interpreted. This passage forms part of the Amos–Numbers midrash in manuscript A of CD and is absent from manuscript B. We will return to the problem of the divergences between manuscripts A and B of the mediaeval text in Chapter 7 below. CD 7.14-15 reads,

> As he said, 'I will exile the *sikkuth* of your king and the *kiyyun* of your images from my tent to Damascus.'

The citation differs from the Masoretic text in two respects. First, elements from Amos 5.26a have been transposed into Amos 5.27a. Secondly, whereas the Masoretic text reads 'beyond Damascus', CD 7.15 has 'from my tent to Damascus'. In the interpretation that follows the ancient exegete emphasizes that this prophetic passage describes God's act of saving the faithful and establishing their place of exile in Damascus. As Vermes has clearly demonstrated, on the ancient exegete's reading of Amos 5.26-27, and probably also under the influence of Zech. 9.1, 'Damascus' is a scriptural cipher that refers to the divinely ordained place of exile of the community wherever this place may be geographically (Vermes 1973: 43-49; see also Milikowsky 1982). As Vermes puts it,

> If they did travel to Damascus, it was because God had decreed and foretold that they would live in that area. If, in fact, they went somewhere else, they still called this place 'the land of Damascus', because their exegesis of Holy Scripture obliged them to do so (Vermes 1973: 44).

Thus, according to CD 7.14-18 'Damascus' is an exegetical term derived from Amos 5.26-27 to describe the community's place of exile where they faithfully devote themselves to the study of the law. This place could well have been Qumran in the minds of those who settled at Qumran and read and/or copied the Damascus Document there. This is not to say that the cipher was not understood and interpreted differently by other ancient interpreters or even by the same group of people at different times in their history. Because of the allusive nature of the references to Damascus it is impossible to be certain how it was interpreted, and this uncertainty has left its mark on the contemporary scholarly debate.

3. The History of the Community(ies)

In attempts at writing a history of the community(ies) described in the Damascus Document, research has focused on two areas of enquiry: the chronological references contained within the document and the identification of various cryptically described individuals and groups. I will deal with each of these in turn.

3.1. The chronological references in the Damascus Document

The Damascus Document comprises a number of chronological references that give an impression, at first sight, of providing precise dates for key events in the history of the community. Thus, CD 1.5-6 places the emergence of a movement of pious Jews 'three hundred and ninety years' after the capture of Jerusalem by Nebuchadnezzar. The position adopted here presupposes translating CD 1.5-6, along with the majority of scholars, as 'three hundred and ninety years *after* he had given them into the hand of Nebuchadnezzar, king of Babylon'. This translation has been questioned by some (Ginzberg 1976: 210-11, 258-60; Rabinowitz 1954). Both Ginzberg and Rabinowitz understand the account in CD 1 as recounting biblical history rather than describing the emergence of a community. Ginzberg argues that the 390 years ended in 721 BCE with the destruction of Samaria. Rabinowitz, on the other hand, proposes that the period in question ended with the exile in 587 BCE rather than began there. Rabinowitz's view is favoured also by A. Jaubert (1958). Neither of these positions has found wide support, however. A further chronological reference occurs in CD 1.9-10 where we are told that the new movement went through a period of uncertainty until the arrival of a teacher of righteousness after 'twenty years'. Finally, according to CD 20.13-15 'forty years' will pass from the death of the teacher until the unfolding of the messianic era, cf. also CD 19.35–20.1. A sizeable group of commentators argue that one or both chronological figures in CD 1 are intrusive and best regarded as secondary glosses (Boyce 1990; Callaway 1988: 130; Charles 1977: II, 800; Davies 1983: 66, 199; Stegemann 1971: 132-33; see also Knibb 1987: 20). In spite of these suspicions about the secondary character of these figures and their widely recognized symbolic significance, most interpreters take them to be nevertheless approximately reliable historically. In particular, the 'three hundred and ninety years' are derived from Ezek. 4.5 and the 'forty years' correspond to the period which the Israelites spent in the wilderness (see Knibb 1987: 73-74). In sum, the chronological data in the Damascus Document is largely based on scripture and should not be treated as factual, historical information. In practice, however, CD 1 places the emergence of a reform movement in the first half of the second century BCE which results in a chronology that is approximately credible on other grounds.

3.2. Identification of Various Individuals and Groups

The identification of and interrelationship between the various individuals and groups referred to by means of nicknames in D has received a great deal of scholarly attention, and these nicknames are largely responsible for the document's 'esoteric mode of communication' (Ginzberg 1976: 257). We encountered this characteristic feature already in the discussion of the references to 'Damascus' above. An important obstacle for historical interpretations of D, and related to the use of nicknames which are usually scripturally based, is the pronounced biblical dictum of the narrative. The accounts of the community's history are saturated with biblical language so that biblical history and the fate of historical Israel blend into one with the community's history. This strong scriptural influence on the community's self-consciousness can be explained partly by their belief that they constituted the true Israel. What is more, the study of scripture played a pivotal part in the life of the community(ies) reflected in the scrolls. This is apparent from statements such as 1QS 6.6-8 which refers to nightly sessions of reading scripture, the presence of the biblical commentaries, and not least the biblical dictum of much of their literature including the Damascus Document. The study of scripture was a fundamental aspect of the quest for enlightenment about God's dealings with the community in the past, present, and future. This latter characteristic inevitably favoured a biblical framework and terminology in order to express reflections on the community's past.

Reconstruction of the history of the community(ies) reflected in the scrolls, an endeavour in which the evidence of the Damascus Document plays an important part, has centred for a long time on personalities, and a dominant avenue of research have been attempts at identifying the teacher of righteousness and his enemies. Influential in setting this trend was the study of G. Jeremias and the work by Jeremias's pupil H. Stegemann (Jeremias 1963; Stegemann 1971).

The identification of the teacher of righteousness, in particular, has aroused a great deal of scholarly interest. This individual is mentioned in the Damascus Document in CD 1.11; 20.32. A related figure is referred to as 'the one who will teach righteousness' in CD 6.11 and as 'the unique teacher' in CD 20.1, 14. The underlying Hebrew expression of the latter designation is often emended to read 'the teacher of the community'. The identification of the teacher of righteousness is, moreover, closely linked to the question of the identification of his contemporary rival, the wicked priest, mentioned in the *pesharim*. On the basis of the statements about the wicked priest in the *pesharim* this individual is usually identified with one or several Hasmonean rulers, such as Jonathan (Jeremias 1963; Knibb 1979; Milik 1959; Murphy-O'Connor 1974; Stegemann 1971; Vermes 1981 and others) or Simon (Cross 1995). An influential reconstruction of the community's early history has been offered by Vermes, and his conclusions have been accepted by the majority of scholars (Vermes 1981). The identification of the wicked priest leads Vermes to the dates for his contemporary opponent, the teacher of righteousness. All this points to the mid-second century for the emergence of the teacher and the sect. These results are then related to CD 1 and the Qumran settlement. On the basis of his analysis of the *pesharim*, H. Stegemann argues that the teacher of righteousness was high priest during the so-called Intersacerdotium, the period 159–152 BCE during which the high priestly office was supposedly vacant (Stegemann 1971). According to this hypothesis the teacher's high priestly office was usurped by Jonathan in 152 BCE. In the *pesharim* the titular use of 'the priest' is applied to both the teacher of righteousness and the wicked priest and refers, in Stegemann's view, to the high priest. Whereas some are sympathetic to Stegemann's argument (Knibb 1979: 299-300; Murphy-O'Connor 1974: 229), it has been questioned by others (Charlesworth 1980: 222; Collins 1989; Wise 1990b).

The overall conclusion of an analysis along these lines, which is still a dominant view, is that it was the teacher of righteousness, a Zadokite former high priest who had been removed from office by the Maccabee Jonathan in 152 BCE, who brought about the break between the community and the Jerusalem temple. This hypothesis was then combined with the archaeological evidence provided by the chief excavator of the site, R. de Vaux, who suggested a mid-second-century date for the beginning of the communal occupation of the Qumran settlement (de Vaux 1973). Such a combination of archaeological and literary evidence to form a synthesis is methodologically problematic since it encourages reading the results of one's study of one body of evidence into one's perception of the other. It is methodologically preferable to analyse the texts and the archaeological remains in their own right before attempting a synthesis. For an analogous debate concerning the methodological pitfalls of engaging in 'biblical archaeology', see the contribution by W.G. Dever in *Israelite and Judaean History* (Hayes and Miller 1977: 71-73). A tongue-in-cheek critique of Qumran archaeology has been offered by P.R. Davies (1988b). On the basis of the archaeological remains, particularly the coins, a mid-second-century date for the beginning of the communal use of the site as proposed by de Vaux (his phase Ia) has been forcefully challenged (Laperrousaz 1976: 28-33). Moreover, building on her analysis of the pottery as well as the numismatic evidence, J. Magness has recently proclaimed 'I do not believe that de Vaux's Period Ia existed', and proposes the onset of the first century BCE for the beginning of the communal occupation of the site (1998: 64-65). Thus, the long-established grand synthesis of Qumran origins that relied on a combination of archaeological and literary evidence is no longer tenable. This collapse of the grand synthesis has important implications which are only now being assessed.

A synthesis of texts and archaeology was paralleled by another synthesis that characterized much Qumran research until recently, and that is the endeavour to offer a synthesis of the statements in different texts. The methodological danger of this approach is again one of harmonization. Thus, although the wicked priest is not mentioned in the Damascus Document, scholars have for a long time interpreted the accounts in D on the basis of their understanding of the *pesharim*, a tendency rejected by P.R. Davies (1983: 2, 14-16). Thus Davies notes,

> The real task, of course, is not to fabricate ingenious reconciliations of discrepant data, nor to distort the balance of agreement and disagreement between CD and the documents of the Qumran community, but to formulate an account of the literary evidence which is exegetically sound and which does justice to *both* similarities *and* differences between CD and the Qumran scrolls (1983: 19).

If we heed Davies's advice and focus on the evidence of the Damascus Document itself it soon becomes clear that even the complex picture painted by this limited evidence is exceedingly difficult to interpret. Thus, according to CD 1.11 the teacher of righteousness is a figure of the past who joins an already existing movement 20 years after its inception. In CD 6.11, by contrast, the teacher is apparently a future figure whereas an individual referred to as the interpreter of the law is associated with the beginnings of a movement in CD 6.7. The latter individual is again referred to in CD 7.18-19 where he appears to be a future figure (cf. 4QFlor 1.11), although the Hebrew underlying the statement 'who will come to Damascus' describing his expected arrival is ambiguous and could also be rendered 'who came to Damascus'. Most scholars argue that the teacher of righteousness and the interpreter of the law of CD 6.7 are one and the same person (Collins 1995: 103-104; Knibb 1987: 49; Murphy-O'Connor 1974: 220; Schechter 1910: xiii). R.H. Charles, on the other hand, thinks the interpreter of the law was an earlier leading figure who led the group's temporary migration to Damascus and was later succeeded by the teacher after the group's return to Palestine (1977: II, 792-93). In his dissertation M. Boyce agrees with those who take the titles teacher of righteousness and interpreter of the law to refer to one and the same figure (1988). He adds to this debate that on his analysis the author of the poetry in the Admonition used the title teacher of righteousness whereas the midrashic sections display a preference for the title interpreter of the law. CD 19.35–20.1; 20.14 mention the death of the teacher which indicates that the Damascus Document in its final form was compiled after the teacher's death. A different view which argues that the Hebrew *he'aseph* refers not to the death of the teacher but to his gathering the community for an assembly has been put forward by B.Z. Wacholder (1988). A convincing refutation of Wacholder's proposal was recently offered by J.A. Fitzmyer (2000).

The reference to the expectation 'at the end of days' of 'one who will teach righteousness' in CD 6.11 lies at the heart of P.R. Davies's interpretation of the references to the teacher in the Damascus Document (1983: 119-25, 1988a). Davies argues that the community at one time expected a messianic teacher as indicated by CD 6.11, and that the historical teacher referred to in CD 1.11 should be understood as an individual who made claims to this messianic title. His arrival led to a split among the Essenes between those who accepted his messianic claims and those who did not. Davies's hypothesis has been accepted by Murphy-O'Connor (1985: 240-44) and Wise (1990a: 184). Collins and Knibb, on the other hand, have questioned the plausibility of this hypothesis (Collins 1995: 102-104; Knibb 1990). Davies further argues, as part of his literary analysis of the Admonition, that the reference to the teacher in CD 1.11 is a secondary addition (1983: 63-64, 200). This view has been challenged by Boyce (1990) who emphasizes that it emerges from his analysis of the poetry of CD 1 that the reference to the teacher in CD 1.11 forms an integral part of the text.

The Admonition further describes opponents of the community in veiled terms. The individual referred to as 'the scoffer' in CD 1.14 is often thought to be the same person labelled 'the liar' in CD 20.15, cf. also CD 8.13 par. 19.25-26 and 20.11. This figure is commonly taken to be the leader of a rival group. The document further polemicizes against a group referred to as 'the builders of the wall' (cf. CD 4.19; 8.12 par. 19.24-25; 8.18 par. 19.31), an expression based on Ezek. 13.10. These examples may suffice to illustrate the allusive nature of the references to the community's history in the Damascus Document.

In the most recent phase of Qumran studies there has been something of a shift away from considering personality clashes as the central force in separating one group from another to a recognition of the central importance of legal disputes in the formation of different groups. This shift has been provoked to a large extent by the recent publication of *Miqsat Ma'ase ha-Torah* (4QMMT), a work that seems to indicate that it was issues of legal interpretation (halakhah) that lay at the heart of the disputes between various groups rather than rivalries between individual priests. Already prior to the publication of 4QMMT, Davies offered an assessment along similar lines (1990: 504). However, perhaps predictably, some would relate the personalities of the wicked priest and the teacher of righteousness also to MMT by identifying the former with the hypothetical addressee and arguing that the latter was the sender of MMT. The recent publication of 4QMMT is only one of several factors that have led to an increased interest in and a recognition of the important role played by Jewish legal interpretation in the scrolls, a topic that will be the subject of the next chapter.

Further Reading

On the Pharisaic identification

Ginzberg, L.
  1976 (1922) *An Unknown Jewish Sect* (New York City: Jewish Theological Seminary of America).

Rabin, C.
  1957 *Qumran Studies* (Oxford: Oxford University Press).

Vermes, G.
  1994 *The Dead Sea Scrolls: Qumran in Perspective* (London: SCM Press, rev. 3rd edn): 104-107.

On the Sadducean identification

Charles, R.H.
    1977 (1913)   *The Apocrypha and Pseudepigrapha of the Old Testament in English with
                   Introductions and Critical and Explanatory Notes to the Several Books* (2 vols.;
                   Oxford: Clarendon): II, 785-834.
Schiffman, L.H.
    1990   'The New Halakhic Letter (4QMMT) and the Origins of the Dead Sea
                   Sect', *BA* 53: 64-73.
    1993   'The Sadducean Origins of the Dead Sea Scroll Sect', in H. Shanks (ed.),
                   Understanding the Dead Sea Scrolls (London: SPCK): 35-49.
For a critique, see:
Davies, P.R.
    1996   'Sadducees in the Dead Sea Scrolls', in *idem, Sects and Scrolls: Essays on Qum-
                   ran and Related Topics* (South Florida Studies in the History of Judaism,
                   134; Atlanta: Scholars Press): 127-38.
Fitzmyer, J.A.
    1995   'The Qumran Community: Essene or Sadducean?', *HeyJ* 36: 467-76.
VanderKam, J.C.
    1993   'The People of the Dead Sea Scrolls: Essenes or Sadducees?', in H. Shanks
                   (ed.), *Understanding the Dead Sea Scrolls* (London: SPCK): 50-62.
Vermes, G.
    1994   *The Dead Sea Scrolls: Qumran in Perspective* (London: SCM Press, rev. 3rd
                   edn): 102-104.

On the Essene identification

Albright, W.F., and C.S. Mann
    1969   'Qumran and the Essenes: Geography, Chronology, and Identification of the
                   Sect', in M. Black (ed.), *The Scrolls and Christianity: Historical and Theo-
                   logical Significance* (London: SPCK): 11-25.
Beall, T.S.
    1988   *Josephus' Description of the Essenes Illustrated by the Dead Sea Scrolls* (SNTSMS,
                   58; Cambridge: Cambridge University Press).
Callaway, P.R.
    1988   *The History of the Qumran Community: An Investigation* (JSOTSup, 3; Shef-
                   field: JSOT Press): 63-87.
Cross, F.M.
    1995   *The Ancient Library of Qumran* (The Biblical Seminar, 30; Sheffield: Shef-
                   field Academic Press, rev. 3rd edn): 54-87.
Dimant, D.
    1984   'Qumran Sectarian Literature', in M.E. Stone (ed.), *Jewish Writings of the
                   Second Temple Period: Apocrypha, Pseudepigrapha, Qumran Sectarian Writ-
                   ings, Philo, Josephus* (CRINT, 2.II; Philadelphia: Fortress Press; Assen: Van
                   Gorcum): 483-550, esp. 485-87.
Dupont-Sommer, A.
    1961   *The Essene Writings from Qumran* (ET, G. Vermes; Oxford: Blackwell).
Goodman, M.D.
    1995   'A Note on the Qumran Sectarians, the Essenes and Josephus', *JJS* 46: 161-
                   66.
Milik, J.T.
    1959   *Ten Years of Discovery in the Wilderness of Judaea* (ET, J. Strugnell; London:
                   SCM Press): 44-98.

Schürer, E., G. Vermes, F. Millar, and M. Black
  1979   *The History of the Jewish People in the Age of Jesus Christ* (3 vols.; Edinburgh: T. & T. Clark): II, 555-97.
Stegemann, H.
  1992   'The Qumran Essenes—Local Members of the Main Jewish Union in Late Second Temple Times', in J. Trebolle Barrera and L. Vegas Montaner (eds.), *The Madrid Qumran Congress: Proceedings of the International Congress on the Dead Sea Scrolls, Madrid 18–21 March 1991* (STDJ, 11; 2 vols.; Leiden: E.J. Brill): I, 83-166.
  1998a   *The Library of Qumran: On the Essenes, Qumran, John the Baptist, and Jesus* (Grand Rapids: Eerdmans; Leiden: E.J. Brill): 139-210.
VanderKam, J.C.
  1994a   *The Dead Sea Scrolls Today* (London: SPCK): 71-98.
Vermes, G.
  1981   'The Essenes and History', *JJS* 32: 18-31.
  1994   *The Dead Sea Scrolls: Qumran in Perspective* (London: SCM Press, rev. 3rd edn): 111-24.
Vermes G., and M.D. Goodman.
  1989   *The Essenes: According to the Classical Sources* (Oxford Centre Textbooks, 1; Sheffield: JSOT Press).

On community origins and early history

Boyce, M.
  1990   'The Poetry of the *Damascus Document* and its Bearing on the Origin of the Qumran Sect', *RevQ* 14: 615-28.
Callaway, P.R.
  1988   *The History of the Qumran Community: An Investigation* (JSOTSup, 3; Sheffield: JSOT Press): 89-133.
Charlesworth, J.H.
  1980   'The Origin and Subsequent History of the Authors of the Dead Sea Scrolls: Four Transitional Phases Among the Qumran Essenes', *RevQ* 10: 213-33.
Collins, J.J.
  1989   'The Origin of the Qumran Community: A Review of the Evidence', in M.P. Horgan and P.J. Kobelski (eds.), *To Touch the Text: Biblical and Related Studies in Honor of Joseph A. Fitzmyer* (New York: Crossroad): 159-78.
  1995   *The Scepter and the Star: The Messiahs of the Dead Sea Scrolls and Other Ancient Literature* (New York: Doubleday): 102-104.
  1997   *Apocalypticism in the Dead Sea Scrolls* (The Literature of the Dead Sea Scrolls; London: Routledge): 66-67.
Cross, F.M.
  1995   *The Ancient Library of Qumran* (The Biblical Seminar, 30; Sheffield: Sheffield Academic Press, rev. 3rd edn): 88-120.
Davies, P.R.
  1977   'Ḥasidim in the Maccabean Period', *JJS* 28: 127-40.
  1987   *Behind the Essenes: History and Ideology in the Dead Sea Scrolls* (BJS, 94; Atlanta: Scholars Press): 107-34.
  1988a   'The Teacher of Righteousness and the "End of Days"', *RevQ* 13: 313-17.
  1990   'The Birthplace of the Essenes: Where is "Damascus"?', *RevQ* 14: 503-19.
Dimant, D.
  1984   'Qumran Sectarian Literature', in M.E. Stone (ed.), *Jewish Writings of the Second Temple Period: Apocrypha, Pseudepigrapha, Qumran Sectarian Writ-*

ings, Philo, Josephus (CRINT, 2.II; Philadelphia: Fortress Press; Assen: Van Gorcum): 483-550, esp. 542-47.

Fitzmyer, J.A., SJ
2000   'The Gathering in of the Teacher of the Community', in *idem, The Dead Sea Scrolls and Christian Origins* (Studies in the Dead Sea Scrolls and Related Literaure; Grand Rapids: Eerdmans): 261-65.

García Martínez, F.
1988   'Qumran Origins and Early History: A Groningen Hypothesis', *Folia Orientalia* 25: 113-36.

García Martínez, F., and J. Trebolle Barrera
1995   *The People of the Dead Sea Scrolls: Their Writings, Beliefs and Practices* (Leiden: E.J. Brill): 77-96.

Hempel, C.
1999   'Community Origins in the Damascus Document in the Light of Recent Scholarship', in D.W. Parry and E.C. Ulrich (eds.), *The Provo International Conference on the Dead Sea Scrolls: Technological Innovations, New Texts, and Reformulated Issues* (STDJ, 30; Leiden: E.J. Brill): 316-29.

Hengel, M.
1981   *Judaism and Hellenism: Studies in their Encounter in Palestine during the Early Hellenistic Period* (London: SCM Press): 175-254.

Iwry, S.
1969   'Was There a Migration to Damascus? The Problem of שבי ישראל', *Eretz Israel* 9: 80-88.

Jaubert, A.
1958   'Le pays de Damas', *RB* 65: 214-48.

Jeremias, G.
1979   *Der Lehrer der Gerechtigkeit* (SUNT, 2; Göttingen: Vandenhoeck & Ruprecht).

Knibb, M.A.
1979   'The Dead Sea Scrolls: Reflections on some Recent Publications', *Expository Times* 90: 294-300.
1983   'Exile in the Damascus Document', *JSOT* 25: 99-117.
1989   *Jubilees and the Origins of the Qumran Community: An Inaugural Lecture* (London: King's College).
1990   'The Teacher of Righteousness—A Messianic Title?', in P.R. Davies and R.T. White (eds.), *A Tribute to Geza Vermes. Essays on Jewish and Christian Literature and History* (JSOTSup, 100; Sheffield: JSOT Press): 51-65.

Laato, A.
1992   'The Chronology in the *Damascus Document* of Qumran', *RevQ* 15: 607-609.

Milik, J.T.
1959   *Ten Years of Discovery in the Wilderness of Judaea* (ET, J. Strugnell; London: SCM Press): 80-85.

Milikowsky, C.
1982   'Again: *Damascus* in Damascus Document and Rabbinic Literature', *RevQ* 11: 97-106.

Murphy-O'Connor, J.
1974   'The Essenes and their History', *RB* 81: 215-44.
1985   'The *Damascus Document* Revisited', *RB* 92: 223-46.

Nickelsburg, G.W.
    1986   '*1 Enoch* and Qumran Origins: The State of the Question and Some Prospects for Answers', in K.H. Richards (ed.), *Society of Biblical Literature Seminar Papers* (Atlanta: Scholars Press): 341-60.

North, R.
    1955   'The Damascus of Qumran Geography', *PEQ* 87: 34-48.

Rabinowitz, I.
    1954   'A Reconsideration of "Damascus" and "390 Years" in the "Damascus" ("Zadokite") Fragments', *JBL* 73: 11-35.

Stegemann, H.
    1971   *Die Entstehung der Qumrangemeinde* (Bonn: privately published).

Stemberger, G.
    1995   *Jewish Contemporaries of Jesus: Pharisees, Sadducees, Essenes* (Minneapolis: Fortress Press): 97-102.

Stone, M.E.
    1991   'Enoch, Aramaic Levi and Sectarian Origins', in *idem, Selected Studies in Pseudepigrapha and Apocrypha: With Special Reference to the Armenian Tradition* (SVTP, 9; Leiden: E.J. Brill): 247-58.

Strickert, F.
    1986   'Damascus Document VII, 10-20 and Qumran Messianic Expectation', *RevQ* 12: 327-49.

VanderKam, J.C.
    1999   'Identity and History of the Community', in P.W. Flint and J.C. VanderKam (eds.), *The Dead Sea Scrolls after Fifty Years: A Comprehensive Assessment* (2 vols.; Leiden: E.J. Brill): II, 487-533.

Vermes, G.
    1981   'The Essenes and History', *JJS* 32: 18-31.
    1994   *The Dead Sea Scrolls: Qumran in Perspective* (London: SCM Press, rev. 3rd edn): 125-41.

Wacholder, B.Z.
    1988   'Does Qumran Record the Death of the *Moreh*? The Meaning of *he'aseph* in *Damascus Covenant* XIX, 35, XX, 14', *RevQ* 13: 323-30.

Wise, M.O.
    1990a   *A Critical Study of the Temple Scroll from Qumran Cave 11* (Studies in Ancient Oriental Civilization, 49; Chicago: The Oriental Institute of the University of Chicago): 184.
    1990b   'The Teacher of Righteousness and the High Priest of the Intersacerdotium: Two Approaches', *RevQ* 14: 587-613.

van der Woude, A.S.
    1998   'Fifty Years of Qumran Research', in P.W. Flint and J.C. VanderKam (eds.), *The Dead Sea Scrolls after Fifty Years: A Comprehensive Assessment* (2 vols.; Leiden: E.J. Brill): I, 1-45, esp. 28-35.

On the profound influence of scripture

Campbell, J.G.
    1995   *The Use of Scripture in the Damascus Document* (BZAW, 228; Berlin: de Gruyter).

Talmon, S.
    1989   *The World of Qumran from Within: Collected Studies* (Jerusalem: Magnes Press): 11-52.

On Qumran archaeology

Callaway, P.R.

    1988   *The History of the Qumran Community: An Investigation* (JSOTSup, 3; Sheffield: JSOT Press): 29-51.

Davies, P.R.

    1988b   'How Not to Do Archaeology: The Story of Qumran', *BA* 51: 203-207.

Laperrousaz, E.-M.

    1976   *Qoumrân: L'établissement essénien des bords de la Mer Morte. Histoire et archéologie du site* (Paris: A. & J. Picard).

Magness, J.

    1998   'Qumran Archaeology: Past Perspectives and Future Prospects', in P.W. Flint and J.C. VanderKam (eds.), *The Dead Sea Scrolls after Fifty Years: A Comprehensive Assessment* (2 vols.; Leiden: E.J. Brill): I, 47-77.

de Vaux, R.

    1973   *Archaeology and the Dead Sea Scrolls* (London: Oxford University Press).

6

THE LAWS—A STORY OF NEGLECT AND REDISCOVERY

One of the most significant developments in recent Qumran studies has been the recognition of the central place occupied by legal issues in the Qumran texts. An important turning point was Y. Yadin's publication of the Temple Scroll (1983). More recently, the publication of and pre-publication debate centred on 4QMMT have helped to place issues of Jewish legal interpretation in the forefront of scholarly debates. The recent full publication of the Cave 4 manuscripts of the Damascus Document has, moreover, changed our perception of the nature of this work. Whereas it was the Admonition that has been the dominant focus of scholarly attention until recently, it is now clear that the bulk of the document is of a legal nature (Baumgarten 1992e). An important exception in this regard is the work of L. Ginzberg (1976 [1922]). His conviction that the halakhic position advocated in the Laws of CD is a Pharisaic one has not found many followers. However, Ginzberg deserves to be credited with emphasizing the importance of halakhah in the formation of sects long before this was fashionable. Consider, for instance, the following observation:

> Accordingly, for the correct understanding of the circle in which the fragments that here engage our attention originated, the Halakah contained in them is much more important than their theological position. (Ginzberg 1976: 105).

At the time of its original formulation and for decades to come Ginzberg's evaluation of the centrality of halakhah remained a cry in the wilderness. Only the subsequent publication of important legal texts and recent shifts in scholarly interests have proved him right.

The relationship between the Laws and the Admonition is an area that will have to be re-evaluated in the light of the recent full publication of all the texts. Let me just make a number of brief observations here. The opinion expressed by C. Rabin and subsequently by H. Stegemann that the Admonition and the Laws do not belong to the same composition is no longer tenable in the light of the evidence from Qumran Cave 4 (Rabin 1954, 1958, Stegemann 1990). Thus, 4QD[a, b, c, d, e, f] contain material paralleled in the Admonition and the Laws of CD whereas 4QD[g, h] comprise legal material not preserved in CD.

An important difference between the Admonition and the bulk of the Laws is the lack of polemics in the Laws. This led S. Schechter to observe already in the *editio princeps*, that the document '…in its Hagada, is largely polemical, whilst its Halacha affords little else than mere statements'. (1910: xviii; see further Baumgarten 1992e: 56; Hempel 1998: 18-20; Knibb 1994: 153). The Laws also lack the historical perspective so central in the Admonition (see Hempel 1998: 80-81). What is more, the nicknames and ciphers that occupy a central place in the Admonition are absent in the legal part of the document. Instead, community functionaries not mentioned in the Admonition, such as *maskil* (wise leader, instructor) and *mebaqqer* (overseer), play an important role. What is more, just as it is widely recognized that the historical parts of the Damascus Document are heavily based on scripture, a profound scriptural influence on a sizeable portion of the Laws can also be identified (Hempel 1998: 36-38, 191). Finally, the presence of remnants of additional admonitory material following the catalogue of transgressions in 4QD[e] may necessitate a radical reassessment of the overall structure of the document.

As we saw, the Laws of the Damascus Document attracted only a fraction of the scholarly attention lavished on the Admonition. One area where the legal part of the Damascus Document has entered the debate on the history of the community is in the form of the argument put forward by S. Iwry and endorsed by J. Murphy-O'Connor and H. Stegemann that the Laws reflect a community living in a gentile environment, either in Syria as suggested by Iwry (1969: 85) and Stegemann (1992: 146-47) or the Babylonian exile, so Murphy-O'Connor (1974). In support of their argument these scholars have drawn attention to those parts of the Laws that make reference to gentiles and dealings between Jews and gentiles. M.A. Knibb has questioned this conclusion and drawn attention to the presence of stipulations referring to the Jerusalem temple (CD 12.1-2) and the bringing of sacrifices (CD 11.17-21), which suggest a Palestinian setting for the Laws (1983: 104-105). He further stresses that it is quite probable that interaction between Jews and gentiles left a mark on the legislation of a community at home in a Palestinian context. Moreover, L.H. Schiffman (1983b) has examined the section dealing with relations with gentiles in CD 12.6-11 and compared it to rabbinic literature. In the course of this comparison he notes numerous parallels. Schiffman's study shows that restrictions on relations between Jews and gentiles of the kind reflected in CD 12.6-11 were a topic of concern in Jewish legal debates in subsequent centuries. It may, therefore, be premature to suppose that such issues were raised only by communities living in the diaspora. Recently J.M. Baumgarten has drawn attention to two passages in the now published Cave 4 material and their relevance to this ongoing debate (1996: 9-10). Firstly, as restored and interpreted by Baumgarten, 4QD^a 6 iv 1-3 stipulates that the law of the fourth-year produce applied not only in Palestine but also in the diaspora. Secondly, 4QD^a 5 ii 5 refers to the ritual impurity of a priest who has been taken captive by gentiles, and 4QD^a 5 ii 8 may refer to priests who depart to serve in another country although the latter passage is only partially preserved (see Baumgarten 1996: 49-51). We may recall, finally, the prohibition of spending the sabbath in the vicinity of gentiles which is found in CD 11.14-15 par. 4QD^f 5 i 9 but lacking in 4QD^e 6 v 8. Neither side of this argument is able to draw on a conclusive piece of evidence, and this debate is likely to continue.

The legal part of D, as emerges from the outline in Chapter 3 above, comprises a variety of material dealing with topics such as oaths, witnesses, purity, relations with gentiles, sabbath, agriculture, priests, organizational matters, and community discipline. This collection is unusual in that it combines general halakhic topoi such as rules on sabbath observance and tithing with matters of communal organization.

Further Reading

Baumgarten, J, M.

1992e   'The Laws of the Damascus Document in Current Research', in M. Broshi (ed.), *The Damascus Document Reconsidered* (Jerusalem: Israel Exploration Society, The Shrine of the Book, Israel Museum): 51-62.

1996   *Qumran Cave 4. XIII. The Damascus Document (4Q266-273)* (DJD, 18; Oxford: Clarendon).

Ginzberg, L.

1976 (1922)   *An Unknown Jewish Sect* (New York: Jewish Theological Seminary of America).

Hempel, C.

1998   *The Laws of the Damascus Document: Sources, Traditions and Redaction* (STDJ, 29; Leiden: E.J. Brill).

Iwry, S.

1969   'Was There a Migration to Damascus? The Problem of שבי ישראל', *Eretz Israel* 9: 80-88.

Knibb, M.A.

1983   'Exile in the Damascus Document', *JSOT* 25: 99-117.

1994   'The Place of the Damascus Document', in M.O. Wise, N. Golb, J.J. Collins, and D.G. Pardee (eds.), *Methods of Investigation of the Dead Sea Scrolls and the Khirbet Qumran Site: Present Realities and Future Prospects* (ANYAS, 722; New York: New York Academy of Sciences): 149-62.

Murphy-O'Connor, J.
    1974   'The Essenes and their History', *RB* 81: 215-44.
Rabin, C.
    1958   *The Zadokite Documents*. I. *The Admonition*. II. *The Laws* (Oxford: Claren-
                don, rev. 2nd edn).
Schechter, S.
    1910   *Documents of Jewish Sectaries*. I. *Fragments of a Zadokite Work* (Cambridge:
                Cambridge University Press).
Schiffman, L.H.
    1983b   'Legislation Concerning Relations with Non-Jews in the *Zadokite Fragments*
                and in Tannaitic Literature', *RevQ* 11: 379-89.
Stegemann, H.
    1990   'Das Gesetzeskorpus der "Damaskusschrift" (CD IX-XVI)', *RevQ* 14: 409-
                34.
    1992   'The Qumran Essenes—Local Members of the Main Jewish Union in Late
                Second Temple Times', in J. Trebolle Barrera and L. Vegas Montaner (eds.),
                *The Madrid Qumran Congress: Proceedings of the International Congress on the
                Dead Sea Scrolls, Madrid 18–21 March 1991* (STDJ, 11; 2 vols.; Leiden: E.J.
                Brill): I, 83-166.

7

FURTHER ISSUES FACING THE STUDENT OF THE DAMASCUS DOCUMENT

1. Messianism

The Damascus Document makes reference to a host of messianic figures. One who will teach righteousness at the end of days is expected according to CD 6.10-11. CD 7.18-21 makes reference to the interpreter of the law and the prince of the congregation apparently expected as two future figures, as the reference to Num. 24.17 suggests (see Knibb 1991; Strickert 1986). Moreover, the interpreter of the law appears as a messianic figure in 4QFlor 1.11. The Hebrew of CD 7.18-21 is ambiguous, however, and can also be taken to describe the interpreter of the law as a past figure (Davies 1983: 147; Milikowsky 1982; Murphy-O'Connor 1985: 242). Some have argued that the interpreter of the law and the prince of the congregation should be seen as a priestly and a royal messianic figure respectively (Collins 1995: 114). The expectation of future figures that share the titles of figures whose role in the past is described elsewhere in the document is one of the cruxes of interpreting the Damascus Document. I discussed some of the debates that have arisen on the basis of this complex picture in Chapter 5 above. In a recent treatment of these questions Collins has argued that this overlap between the titles of past and eschatological figures is best seen as indicative of restorative tendencies that characterize expectations of the end in the scrolls. Thus, Collins observes,

> The use of such titles as Interpreter of the Law and Teacher of Righteousness for figures of the historical past and the eschatological future underlines a feature of the eschatology of the Scrolls that has often been noted. This eschatology has a restorative aspect and involves the fulfilment and perfection of the institutions of past and present. (Collins 1995: 112).

Moreover, M.A. Knibb has emphasized the significance of the composite nature of the Damascus Document to account for differences of this kind (1991: 249). It seems likely that both Collins and Knibb provide parts of the answer.

Finally, a host of passages mention the expectation of 'the messiah of Aaron and Israel' (CD 19.10-11; 12.23–13.1; 14.19 par. 4QD^a 10 i 12 and 4QD^d 11 i 2) or 'the messiah from Aaron and from Israel' (CD 19.35–20.1). These references have been the subject of extensive discussion. The references to 'those anointed with his holy spirit' in CD 2.12 and the related expression in CD 6.1 are generally recognized as alluding to the biblical prophets and as such will not concern us here. Some argue that the expression 'messiah of Aaron and Israel' refers to a single messiah (Brooke 1991: 221-24; Knibb 1987: 60). Such a notion is somewhat unusual in the scrolls, and in the past this has led to suggestions that the singular form of the expression in the Damascus Document goes back to a mediaeval correction (Kuhn 1959: 59-60). Since the ancient fragments now confirm the reading of CD the latter view is no longer tenable. Others prefer to understand the singular expression to refer to two messiahs in analogy with 1QS 9.11 where the expression 'the messiahs of Aaron and Israel' occurs in the plural (Collins 1995: 79-83; Dimant 1984: 539-40; Ginzberg 1976: 209-56; VanderKam 1994b: 230). It is interesting to note that one of the manuscripts of the Community Rule from Cave 4, 4QS^e (4Q259), lacks the section that contains the famous reference to 'the prophet and the messiahs of Aaron and Israel' (Alexander and Vermes 1998: 148; Metso 1997: 71-73). The roots of the notion of two messianic figures can be traced to the later prophetic books of the Hebrew Bible, especially Zechariah 4 (cf. Knibb 1987: 139-40; Talmon 1989: 290-93). Those who prefer to take the expression to refer to a single figure have appealed to CD 14.18-19 where the phrase 'the messiah of Aaron and Israel' is followed by a verb in the singular which most naturally means 'he will atone'. A passive translation of the verb along the lines 'atonement will be made' is also possible. However, as J.C. VanderKam has pointed out, the singular form of the verb conforms with the singular form of the noun messiah and sheds little light on the understanding of the larger phrase (1994a: 230). As often stressed by those who argue that the expression refers to two figures, it is difficult to explain why the twofold reference would have been used to refer to a single messiah. It is widely agreed that the two components of this title refer either to the priestly and royal aspects of a single messiah or to two messiahs, one of priestly and the other of royal descent (see Collins 1997: 77-80). Finally, it is noteworthy that the messianic references in the Damascus Document are consistently used in a temporal sense to indicate a turning point in God's dealings with the faithful and the wicked in phrases of the type 'until the coming of the messiah of Aaron and Israel'. It appears that speculation about the role of the messiah(s) in the unfolding of the eschaton is not a concern of the author(s) of the Damascus Document. VanderKam has aptly summarized this characteristic by describing the function of the messianic references in D 'to define a unit of time' (VanderKam 1994b: 229).

2. The Divergences between Manuscripts A and B

Because a number of the most important messianic references occur in that part of the Damascus Document where the two mediaeval manuscripts diverge it is appropriate to discuss this issue at this point. The texts of both manuscripts in English translation are clearly set out in Knibb's commentary (1987: 59-69). Rabin's edition of 1954 produced a composite text of both versions, arguing that they are two deficient copies of an original. In the second edition of his book, which appeared in 1958, he added an appendix where both versions are produced separately (Rabin 1954, 1958). A number of hypotheses have been put forward to account for the textual differences between both manuscripts, and I will briefly outline the most important of these.

Thus, J. Carmignac (1959) argues that the great majority of divergences between both manuscripts constitute minor scribal variations but he allows also for a small number of deliberate alterations. J. Murphy-O'Connor suggests that the original text consisted of a combination of material from manuscripts A and B, that is CD 7.9b-13a (Isaiah midrash) followed by CD 19.7b-14 (Zechariah–Ezekiel midrash) (Murphy-O'Connor 1971b). He further suggests that the Isaiah midrash was accidentally dropped from manuscript B, and that the Zechariah–Ezekiel midrash was replaced in manuscript A by the Amos–Numbers midrash. He later revised his earlier conclusions and now holds that the Amos–Numbers midrash is original as opposed to the Zechariah–Ezekiel midrash (Murphy-O'Connor 1985). F. Strickert proposes that manuscript A represents the original text whereas manuscript B is the result of a deliberate revision process (1986). We recall that Strickert interprets the reference to Damascus in the Amos–Numbers midrash literally. He further argues that the revision attested by the B-text was concerned to remove this reference to Damascus after the group had now settled at Qumran. This view is somewhat difficult to reconcile with the presence of the Amos–Numbers midrash in both Cave 4 manuscripts that preserve material belonging to this part of the document, that is 4QDᵃ (4Q266) and 4QDᵈ (4Q269). I will return to the Cave 4 evidence at the end of this section. P.R. Davies (1987) maintains that the

Amos–Numbers midrash and the Zechariah–Ezekiel midrash are secondary, and that the latter was inserted into the B-text in order to tone down the military aspects of the messiah. S.A. White attempts to solve the puzzle by asserting that both the Amos–Numbers midrash and the Zechariah–Ezekiel midrash are original and argues that the shorter text of both manuscripts A and B was caused by two instances of haplography, that is a type of scribal error where the eye of the scribe inadvertently jumped from one similar or identical word or phrase to the next occurrence leaving out the intervening material (White 1987). In White's view the repeated phrases 'were delivered up to the (avenging) sword' in CD 7.13 and 19.13 and 'which is written' in CD 7.10 and 19.7 provoked the scribal errors in this case. G.J. Brooke (1991) proposes a development in the messianic expectations reflected in the document. He maintains that manuscript B and the Laws reflect the beliefs of an early stage characterized by the expectation of a single messiah, 'the messiah of Aaron and Israel'. Stage two is represented by the Amos–Numbers midrash in manuscript A which envisages the coming of two messiahs in line with numerous other texts from Qumran, 'the interpreter of the law' and 'the prince of the congregation'. A third stage, and here Brooke is broadly similar to Davies, is represented by the reinsertion of the Zechariah–Ezekiel midrash attested by manuscript B. Finally, M.A. Knibb (1991) also takes the view that the Amos–Numbers midrash is secondary and argues that it most likely originated independently.

Future studies of this vexed issue will be able to draw on the full Cave 4 evidence. We may observe already that 4QD^a 3 iii-iv largely conforms to manuscript A as does 4QD^d 5 (cf. Baumgarten 1996: 44-45, 128). This was already noted by J.T. Milik (1959: 60 n. 1). However, in 4QD^a 3 iii 25 the partial preservation of the phrase 'as [he has said]' aligns 4QD^a with the text of manuscript B, cf. CD 19.15 over against CD 8.3. On the other hand, 4QD^a 3 iv 2 resembles the reading of CD 8.4. The scant remains of 4QD^d 6 contain material found in both CD 8.5-6 and 19.17-19. When one tries to assess the scholarly hypotheses outlined above in the light of the recently published texts of 4QD^a and 4QD^d it is not at all clear that the new evidence resolves the debate. It is theoretically possible, for example, that the now lost parts of 4QD^a and 4QD^d continued with the Zechariah–Ezekiel midrash (manuscript B) in addition to the fragmentarily preserved Amos–Numbers midrash (manuscript A). It may be that the material reconstruction of the 4QD manuscripts that is being prepared by H. Stegemann and his team in Göttingen will shed more light on this issue. Collins takes the evidence of 4QD^a as speaking against the views of those who hold that the Amos–Numbers midrash is secondary (1995: 82). While taking note of the fact that 4QD^a and 4QD^d attest this material we cannot take it for granted, it seems to me, that ancient copies of a work may not include secondary material.

3. Covenant

The notion of covenant is an important one in the Damascus Document. The term occurs 44 times in the mediaeval and ancient manuscripts not including references that occur in overlapping sections. Covenant terminology is used in a number of different ways. It can be used to refer to the Mosaic covenant as in the phrase 'the covenant with those of former times' in CD 1.4, see also 3.10-11; 4.9; 6.2 par. 4QD^b 2.7; 6Q15 3.5. From the perspective of the Admonition the covenant with pre-exilic Israel has been replaced by the covenant between God and the members of a particular community which is portrayed as the faithful remnant of pre-exilic Israel, cf. for example CD 3.13; 8.17-18 par. 19.31. Moreover, throughout the document, including also its legal part, membership in the community is frequently referred to in covenantal terms, cf. for example CD 2.2; 20.25; 15.5, and a central element of the procedure for admitting new members is swearing the oath of the covenant, cf. CD 15.5b–16.6a par. In the Admonition it is argued that Israel's place in the pre-exilic covenant relationship has been taken by the community in the present time, and it is at times difficult to distinguish whether the text is referring to the Mosaic covenant or the community's covenant. Apparently deliberately ambiguous is the reference of transgressing the covenant in CD 1.20. This passage ostensibly reviews the failings of pre-exilic Israel while implicitly warning contemporary community members not to transgress the community's covenant (Knibb 1987: 24).

CD 6.19; 8.21 par. 19.33-34; 20.12 speak of 'the new covenant in the land of Damascus'. The concept of a new covenant is based on Jer. 31.31, and I have dealt with the intricate problems of interpreting the Damascus imagery in the Admonition in Chapter 5 above. We recall that P.R. Davies argues that the references to the new covenant in CD go back to a Qumranic recension of the document (1983: 176-77). It is remarkable, in any case, that this phrase occurs in a limited number of passages given the preponderance of the unqualified use of the term 'covenant' in the bulk of the document. Davies is surely right when he insists that we should be sensitive to this subtle difference rather than treating it as no more than a stylistic difference. Whether the references to 'the new covenant in the land of Damascus' are adequately described as *Qumranic* is another matter. It is noteworthy that the terminology is not prevalent in key sectarian scrolls. It is conspicuously absent from the Community Rule although the term covenant occurs 32 times in 1QS. To speak, as S. Talmon does, of 'the *yaḥad's* renewed covenant' is somewhat imprecise since the terminology is absent from the Serekh ha-*yaḥad* (Talmon 1994: 22; see further Steudel 1997: 156). It may be best to remain agnostic as to the identity of the ancient exegete who, inspired by Jer. 31.31 and Amos 5.26-27, introduced the idea of a new covenant in the land of Damacus into D. The phrase 'new covenant' without the 'Damascus component' is partially preserved in 1QpHab 2.3. It is safe to say, however, that the idea is confined to a small number of passages both in the scrolls and in the Damascus Document in particular. The unqualified use of the covenant idea, by contrast, pervades both the Damascus Document and the Community Rule.

Two special cases fall outside this picture. Firstly, CD 12.11 prohibits the sale to gentiles of servants who have entered 'the covenant of Abraham'. This seems to refer to the covenant of circumcision in the case of male servants and conversion in the case of females. The context seems to envisage servants who had become proselytes to the Jewish faith rather than members of a particular community, since circumcision is not referred to in any of the passages describing admission into the community. Secondly, in 4QD^d 9.4 par. 4QD^e 5.17 the expression 'holy co[venant]' seems to refer to marriage, although since only the last letter of the Hebrew word for covenant is preserved in both manuscripts we cannot be sure of the reading (cf. Baumgarten 1996: 177).

Apart from the frequent use of the covenant concept throughout the document, a number of scholars have highlighted the importance of the covenant on what one might call a macro-level. That is, a number of attempts have been made to explain the form and purpose of the document as a whole as a work that was composed for liturgical use at a covenant renewal ceremony (Knibb 1987: 14; Vermes 1997: 127). The last portion of the document as now attested by 4QD^a 11.16-18 mentions a gathering of all the inhabitants of the camps 'in the third month', and this is widely understood to refer to a covenant renewal festival (Milik 1959: 116-17). Such a ceremony involved cursing transgressors (4QD^a 11.17) and perhaps also admission into the community (Knibb 1987: 25-26 *ad* CD 2.2; Milik 1959: 116). It is noteworthy, however, that the lengthy description of the admission process in CD 15.5b–16.6a par. appears to envisage a more spontaneous procedure of admission that took place throughout the year. Thus CD 15.7b-8 reads, 'On the day on which he [the candidate wishing to join] speaks to the overseer over the many they shall muster him with the oath of the covenant.' This passage seems to suggest that admission into the community took place on an *ad hoc* basis throughout the year. It is possible, though, that those thus admitted were ceremoniously confirmed as new members in an annual ceremony as well.

K. Baltzer proposes that the literary form of the covenant formulary, a genre widely attested in the Ancient Near East, especially in ancient Hittite treaties, is a useful model for assessing the Damascus Document in its final form (1971: 112-22). In particular, he distinguishes the following components:

> CD 1.1–6.11   Dogmatic Section ('Antecedent History').
> CD 6.11–7.4   Ethical Section.
> CD 7.4ff.   Blessings and Curses.

The conclusion to the Admonition (Baltzer is not explicit on the exact extent of this section), imprecisely referred to as a conclusion to the document as a whole (Baltzer 1971: 117), apparently falls outside the literary form.

> CD 9.1–16.20 Corpus of Legal Stipulations.

Of interest is the Hittite custom of regularly reciting treaties, which might provide a connection between the literary form of the Damascus Document and the annual covenant renewal ceremony alluded to in the last lines of the document (Baltzer 1971: 18). Whether or not one agrees with all the details of Baltzer's analysis, his study provides an important attempt to make sense of the document as a whole as it was known in 1971. An important feature that is explained by the form of the covenant formulary is the mixture of historical and legal components in the document.

Davies (1983) modifies Baltzer's analysis and identifies the form of the covenant formulary in the Admonition without including the Laws in his analysis. The legal component of the covenant formulary is identified by Davies within the Admonition itself in CD 6.11–7.19. A problematic aspect of this approach is that it almost treats the Admonition as an independent composition, although this is never suggested, and that it sheds little light on our understanding of the document as a whole.

4. The Issue of the Calendar

A number of passages in the Damascus Document allude to the issue of observing the correct calendar. As part of a description of community origins, a divine revelation of hidden things which explicitly includes festival observance is mentioned in CD 3.12b-14. It is noteworthy, though, that the calendar does not feature in the other descriptions of communal origins in the Admonition. CD 6.18b-19 par. 4QD^a 3 ii 24-25 and 4QD^d 4 ii 1 includes the issue of the sabbath and the festivals in a list of injunctions. CD 16.2b-4a par. 4QD^e 6 ii 17 and 4QD^f 4 ii 4-5 comprises an explicit reference the book of *Jubilees* as the ultimate authority on calendrical issues, and the fragmentary material preceding the beginning of CD 1.1 preserved in 4QD[a] 2 i 2 par. 4QD[c] 1.4 appears to allude to calendrical matters. Of particular interest is the description of the community's calendric observance as based on a revelation that was *hidden* from Israel at large (CD 3.12-14) or to which Israel was *blind* (CD 16.2-4 par.). We know from a number of texts attested at Qumran that the Qumran community and its ideological predecessors adhered to a 364-day calendar according to which the festivals recurred on the same weekday every year, cf. 4QMMT Section A (4Q394), 4QCommentary on Genesis A (4Q252), *Jubilees, 1 Enoch,* 4QCalendrical Documents (4Q320-330), and 11QPsalms[a] XXVII.6-7 (David's Compositions). The references in the Damascus Document to the ignorance on the part of those outside the community in calendrical matters seem to refer to the observance of a different calendar by other Jews. Until very recently it was customary to speak of two conflicting calendars in terms of a solar calendar, that is the 364-day calendar of the community, and a luni-solar calendar as practised outside the community. In the light of a number of newly available calendrical texts from Cave 4, this clear-cut dichotomy has recently been called into question, and the evidence of the scrolls on calendrical matters emerges as a rather complex web of traditions (Glessmer 1999). A great deal has been written on this topic. However, the larger debate on the complexity of calendric traditions now attested in the scrolls goes beyond the scope of this companion. The pioneering study by S. Talmon entitled 'The Calendar Reckoning of the Sect from the Judaean Desert' (1965) and the recent up-to-date surveys by M. Albani (1997), U. Glessmer (1999), and J.C. VanderKam (1998) can be warmly recommended to those wishing to pursue this issue further.

5. Polygamy and/or Divorce

A halakhic issue that is raised in the famous passage in the Admonition on Israel's ensnarement in the three nets of Belial (CD 4.12b–5.19 par.) has received a fair amount of scholarly attention. We recall that the passage begins with a citation and midrashic exposition of Isa. 24.17 followed by a lengthy commentary on the latter which criticizes a number of contemporary sexual practices. Two of these condemned practices are intercourse with a menstruating woman (CD 5.7) and marrying one's niece (CD 5.7-8). A third criticism is levelled against those who take 'two wives during their [masculine suffix] lifetime' (CD 4.20-21 par.). This formulation has given rise to several interpretations. Some have emphasized that the masculine suffix implies that a man must not have more than one wife during his entire life, and that our passage taken literally prohibits remarriage after a divorce or even after the death of one's wife (Davies 1987: 73-85, 141-43; Murphy-O'Connor 1970: 220). A number of scholars are of the opinion that the passage in question prohibits polygamy only (Vermes 1974) whereas others still have proposed that the passage forbids both polygamy and remarriage after divorce (Winter 1956). With the publication of the Temple Scroll a new piece of evidence has entered this debate. As part of a section known as the Law of the King 11QT^a 57.17-19 includes the following stipulations regarding the king's marital practices:

> And he shall not take upon her another wife, for she alone shall be with him all the days of her life. But should she die, he may take unto himself another (wife) from the house of his father, from his family (translation Yadin 1983: II, 258).

Thus, in the Temple Scroll the position advocated with reference to the king is much less ambiguous than CD 4.20-21 par. Some have argued that this passage from the Temple Scroll strongly supports the view that polygamy was at issue in CD also. Others, by contrast, are critical of using a passage from a different document which, furthermore, deals with the special case of royal marriages to shed light on CD 4.20-21 par. Finally, the possible reference in the very fragmentary material preserved in CD 13.16-17 par. 4QD^a 9 iii 5-4 to the overseer's role in counselling community members who get married or divorced is sometimes appealed to to argue that divorce was apparently considered legitimate in the community behind D. However, in the light of the fragmentary nature of this passage no strong case can be built on it. In sum, a consensus on the interpretation of CD 4.20-21 par. seems as yet out of reach.

Further Reading

On messianism in the Dead Sea Scrolls in general and the Damascus Document in particular

Collins, J.J.

1995   *The Scepter and the Star: The Messiahs of the Dead Sea Scrolls and Other Ancient Literature* (New York: Doubleday): 74-101.

1997   *Apocalypticism in the Dead Sea Scrolls* (The Literature of the Dead Sea Scrolls; London: Routledge): 71-90.

Dimant, D.

1984   'Qumran Sectarian Literature', in M.E. Stone (ed.), *Jewish Writings of the Second Temple Period: Apocrypha, Pseudepigrapha, Qumran Sectarian Writings, Philo, Josephus* (CRINT, 2.II; Philadelphia: Fortress Press; Assen: Van Gorcum): 483-550, esp. 538-42.

Ginzberg, L.
   1976 (1922)   *An Unknown Jewish Sect* (New York: Jewish Theological Seminary of America).
Kuhn, K.G.
   1959   'The Two Messiahs of Aaron and Israel', in K. Stendahl (ed.), *The Scrolls and the New Testament* (London: SCM Press): 54-64.
Milikowsky, C.
   1982   'Again: *Damascus* in Damascus Document and Rabbinic Literature', *RevQ* 11: 97-106.
Schürer, E., G. Vermes, F. Millar, and M. Black
   1979   *The History of the Jewish People in the Age of Jesus Christ* (3 vols.; Edinburgh: T. & T. Clark): II, 550-54.
Talmon, S.
   1989   *The World of Qumran from Within: Collected Studies* (Jerusalem: Magnes Press): 273-300. Although this study is, on the whole, helpful and reliable, the translation of CD 13.20-22 on p. 289 is largely based on reconstructions and should be disregarded as a messianic reference.
VanderKam, J.C.
   1994b   'Messianism in the Scrolls', in E. Ulrich and J.C. VanderKam (eds.), *The Community of the Renewed Covenant: The Notre Dame Symposium on the Dead Sea Scrolls* (Notre Dame: Notre Dame University Press): 211-34.

On the divergences between manuscripts A and B

Brooke, G.J.
   1980   'The Amos–Numbers Midrash (CD 7 13b–8 1a) and Messianic Expectation', *ZAW* 92: 397-404.
   1991   'The Messiah of Aaron in the Damascus Document', *RevQ* 15: 215-30.
Carmignac, J.
   1959   'Comparaison entre les manuscrits "A" et "B" du Document de Damas', *RevQ* 2: 53-67.
Collins, J.J.
   1995   *The Scepter and the Star: The Messiahs of the Dead Sea Scrolls and Other Ancient Literature* (New York: Doubleday): 80-82.
Davies, P.R.
   1983   *The Damascus Covenant: An Interpretation of the 'Damascus Document'* (JSOTSup, 25; Sheffield: Sheffield Academic Press): 143-72.
Knibb, M.A.
   1991   'The Interpretation of Damascus Document VII, 9b-VIII, 2a and XIX, 5b-14', *RevQ* 15: 243-51.
Milik, J.T.
   1959   *Ten Years of Discovery in the Wilderness of Judaea* (ET, J. Strugnell; London: SCM Press).
Murphy-O'Connor, J.
   1971b   'The Original Text of CD 7.9-8.2 = 19.5-14', *HTR* 64: 379-86.
   1985   'The *Damascus Document* Revisited', *RB* 92: 223-46.
Strickert, F.
   1986   'Damascus Document VII, 10-20 and Qumran Messianic Expectation', *RevQ* 12: 327-49.
White, S.A.
   1987   'A Comparison of the "A" and "B" Manuscripts of the Damascus Document', *RevQ* 48: 537-53.

Covenant

Baltzer, K.

1971   *The Covenant Formulary in Old Testament, Jewish, and Early Christian Writings* (ET, D.E. Green; Oxford: Blackwell): 112-22.

Davies, P.R.

1983   *The Damascus Covenant: An Interpretation of the 'Damascus Document'* (JSOTSup, 25; Sheffield: Sheffield Academic Press): 50-53.

Kapelrud, A.S.

1968   'Der Bund in den Qumran-Schriften', in S. Wagner (ed.), *Bibel und Qumran: Beiträge zur Erforschung der Beziehungen zwischen Bibel- und Qumranwissenschaft* (Berlin: Evangelische Haupt-Bibelgesellschaft): 137-49.

Knibb, M.A.

1987   *The Qumran Community* (Cambridge Commentaries on Writings of the Jewish and Christian World 200 BC to AD 200; Cambridge: Cambridge University Press): 14.

Milik, J.T.

1959   *Ten Years of Discovery in the Wilderness of Judaea* (ET, J. Strugnell; London: SCM Press): 113-18.

Steudel, A.

1997   Review of E. Ulrich and J. VanderKam (eds.), *The Community of the Renewed Covenant,* in *RevQ* 18: 156-60, esp. 156.

Talmon, S.

1994   'Qumran Studies: Past, Present, and Future', *JQR* 85: 1-31, esp. 20-22.

Vermes, G.

1997   *The Complete Dead Sea Scrolls in English* (London: Penguin Books): 127.

Calendar

Albani, M.

1997   'Zur Rekonstruktion eines verdrängten Konzepts: Der 364-Tage-Kalender in der gegenwärtigen Forschung', in M. Albani, J. Frey, and A. Lange (eds.), *Studies in the Book of Jubilees* (Texte und Studien zum Antiken Judentum, 65; Tübingen: Mohr Siebeck): 79-125.

Glessmer, U.

1999   'Calendars in the Dead Sea Scrolls', in P.W. Flint and J.C. VanderKam (eds.), *The Dead Sea Scrolls after Fifty Years: A Comprehensive Assessment* (2 vols.; Leiden: E.J. Brill): II, 213-78.

Stegemann, H.

1998a   *The Library of Qumran: On the Essenes, Qumran, John the Baptist, and Jesus* (Grand Rapids: Eerdmans; Leiden: E.J. Brill): 166-74.

Talmon, S.

1965   'The Calendar Reckoning of the Sect from the Judaean Desert', in C. Rabin and Y. Yadin (eds.), *Scripta Hierosolymitana: Publications of the Hebrew University, Jerusalem.* VI. *Aspects of the Dead Sea Scrolls* (Jerusalem: Magnes Press): 162-99.

VanderKam, J.C.

1992   'Calendars: Ancient Israelite and Early Jewish', in *Anchor Bible Dictionary* (6 vols; New York: Doubleday): I, 814-20.

1998   *Calendars in the Dead Sea Scrolls: Measuring Time* (The Literature of the Dead Sea Scrolls; London: Routledge).

On polygamy and/or divorce

Brin, G.

> 1997   'Divorce at Qumran', in M.J. Bernstein, F. García Martínez and J. Kampen (eds.), *Legal Texts and Legal Issues: Proceedings of the Second Meeting of the International Organization for Qumran Studies, Published in Honour of Joseph M. Baumgarten* (STDJ, 23; Leiden: E.J. Brill): 231-44.

Davies, P.R.

> 1987   *Behind the Essenes: History and Ideology in the Dead Sea Scrolls* (BJS, 94; Atlanta: Scholars Press): 73-85, 141-43.

Instone Brewer, D.

> 1998   'Nomological Exegesis in Qumran "Divorce" Texts', *RevQ* 18: 561-79.

Murphy-O'Connor, J.

> 1970   'An Essene Missionary Document? CD II, 14-VI, 1', *RB* 77: 201-29, esp. 220.

Vermes, G.

> 1974   'Sectarian Matrimonial Halakhah in the Damascus Rule', *JJS* 25: 197-202.

Winter, P.

> 1956   'Sadoqite Fragments IV 20, 21 and the Exegesis of Genesis 1:27 in Late Judaism', *ZAW* 68: 71-84.

8

CONCLUDING REFLECTIONS

It has emerged very clearly from the preceding chapters that the Damascus Document is one of the most important texts in the Qumran library. Its importance is indicated both by the large number of copies attested of the document in the Qumran caves (eight in Cave 4 and one in Caves 5 and 6 respectively) as well as by the immense scholarly interest in the issues raised by this text. It is foreseeable that the recent publication of all the Qumran manuscripts of this text as well as the ongoing stream of publications of other new texts from Qumran will provide further stimuli for future research on the issues outlined in this volume.

One area where a considerable amount of research has been undertaken is studies devoted to the composite nature of the document (see Chapter 4 above). A number of studies have attempted to show that both the Admonition and the Laws are composite works, and a case has been made by some that the document has a pre-Qumranic core that was revised by the Qumran community. A related area where there appears to be considerable scope for further research is the study of the literary development of the Damascus Document *as a whole*. It is true that a number of scholars who have in the main dealt with either the Admonition or the Laws have on occasion attempted to include the other part of the document in their hypotheses. However, this is often done in a rather sweeping fashion. It seems desirable now to attempt a synthesis of the growth of the document that takes into account the complexities of each component. By way of concluding this part of the companion, I shall offer a number of reflections on some of the avenues along which such a synthesis might develop on the basis of all the manuscripts and the results of research to date. Firstly, it is noteworthy that the conclusions of Davies overlap with my own inasmuch as we both identify a Qumranic recension or Serekh redaction of originally non-Qumranic material (Davies 1983; Hempel 1998). This may well suggest the presence of a redactional process that spans the whole document. Secondly, my observations on the potential significance of the catalogue of transgressions for our understanding of the literary growth of the Laws deserve to be related to the significance of the list of halakhic prescriptions in CD 6.14b–7.4a (Hempel 2000: 80-84). CD 6.14b–7.4a comprises stipulations that are taken up at greater length in the legal part of D and may shed some light on the growth of the document. Finally, the presence of a call to hearken following the catalogue of transgressions in 4QD^e 2 ii 19 is a crucial passage that may lead us to reassess our evaluation of the literary structure of the whole document. In my analysis of the catalogue of transgressions I argue that what may at first sight look like the conclusion to the catalogue is best taken as a new beginning, introducing a now lost section (Hempel 1998: 163-70). This has been taken further by H. Stegemann in a recent paper. In the course of his oral presentation at the third Orion Symposium Stegemann argued that it is reasonable to suppose that this call to hearken introduced another admonitory discourse along the lines of and of similar length to the discourses familiar from the Admonition such as CD 1.1–2.1. He further observed that in the light of this further admonitory section, the notion of a bipartite division of the document into an Admonition and a section of Laws is no longer to be taken for granted. These observations have not been fully included in the published version of his paper, but cf. Stegemann (2000: 190).

Considerable obstacles to fully understanding the structure of the document as a whole are the fragmentary nature of the ancient manuscripts and the lack of information about the order of much of the Cave 4 material that is not paralleled by the Cairo text. Fortunately, the end of the document from 4QD (cf. 4QD^a 11; 4QD^d 16 [see Stegemann 1998b]; and 4QD^e 7 ii) as well as the fragmentary remains of the beginning (cf. 4QD^a 1 a-b) are preserved in some of the Cave 4 manuscripts. Despite this we are still in the dark as to the exact sequence of much of the intervening material, nor do we know how much further text might have been lost altogether. Yet in spite of these regrettable gaps in our knowledge of the text, the very survival and discovery of so much of this ancient text in the two most ground-breaking discoveries of Jewish manuscripts in the twentieth century is little short of miraculous.

Part II

4Q265 MISCELLANEOUS RULES (*olim* SEREKH DAMASCUS)

Editions and Translations

Editions

Baumgarten, J.M. *et al.*
  1999   *Qumran Cave 4. XXV. Halakhic Texts* (DJD, 35; Oxford: Clarendon Press):
          57-78. This official edition of 4Q265 appeared only after the manuscript of
          the present volume was in press. In the final stages of production I updated
          the references to 4Q265 according to the official edition. It was not possible
          at this late stage, however, to deal with Professor Baumgarten's edition as
          fully as would have been desirable.
García Martínez, F., and E.J.C. Tigchelaar (eds.).
  1997   *The Dead Sea Scrolls Study Edition* (2 vols.; Leiden: E.J. Brill): I, 546-49.
Tov, E., with the collaboration of S. Pfann (ed.).
  1993   *The Dead Sea Scrolls on Microfiche: A Comprehensive Facsimile Edition of the
          Texts from the Judean Desert* (Leiden: E.J. Brill): final photos PAM 43.304-
          43.306.
Wacholder, B.Z., and M.G. Abegg on the basis of the transcriptions of J.T. Milik and others
          (eds.)
  1995   *A Preliminary Edition of the Unpublished Dead Sea Scrolls: The Hebrew and
          Aramaic Texts from Cave Four* (4 fascicles; Washington DC: Biblical Archae-
          ology Society): III, 72-78.

Translations

Abegg, M. Jr, in M. Wise, M. Abegg Jr, and E. Cook
  1996   *The Dead Sea Scrolls. A New Translation* (London: HarperCollins): 278-81.
García Martínez, F.
  1994   *The Dead Sea Scrolls Translated: The Qumran Texts in English* (ET, W.G.E.
          Watson; Leiden: E.J. Brill): 72-73.
Maier, J.
  1996a   *Die Qumran-Essener: Die Texte vom Toten Meer* (UTB, 1863; 3 vols.; Basel:
          Friedrich Reinhardt): II, 215-16.
Vermes, G.
  1997   *The Complete Dead Sea Scrolls in English* (London: Penguin Books): 153-56.

INTRODUCTION

At the time of writing, this fascinating text from Cave 4 has not been officially published. Professor Joseph Baumgarten has recently been entrusted with its publication in the Discoveries in the Judaean Desert Series on the basis of the pioneering work on this text by J.T. Milik, see now Baumgarten (1999) and my remarks on p. 90 above. However, a number of preliminary editions of the Hebrew text as well as English translations have been available for a number of years now. Milik alerted scholars to the existence of this text and gave a brief description of its contents in the 1950s (Milik 1959: 96). The original designation 'Serekh Damascus' was chosen to capture the text's resemblance of the Rule of the Community (or *Serekh* ha Yaḥad), on the one hand, and the *Damascus* Document on the other hand. It is worth stressing, however, that neither the term serekh (rule), a term frequently found in headings in the Community Rule and the Damascus Document, nor Damascus occur anywhere in the preserved fragments of 4Q265.

Most unfortunately, neither an introduction nor a conclusion to this text is preserved, and we cannot even be sure whether 4Q265 was the kind of text that in its final form provided introductory and concluding statements. Since we are lacking virtually all of the linking passages that mark the transition from one apparently disparate portion of text to the next, it is exceedingly difficult to learn much about the form and the function of this text. In one case (4Q265 7.11) the beginning of the line has been left blank apparently to mark the beginning of a new topic. In the absence of further evidence scholars are forced to rely on intelligent suppositions. One important asset for interpreting 4Q265 is, however, the extensive parallels to parts of the Damascus Document and the Community Rule displayed by this text. These parallels have defined scholarly perceptions of 4Q265 from the beginning, and it is clear that the key to our understanding of 4Q265 is its place in the triangle of all three texts. This relationship is, however, complicated by the fact that the relationship between the Damascus Document and the Community Rule is itself highly complex and continues to be keenly debated by scholars. We are, however, at least in the fortunate position of being able to locate the contents of 4Q265 somewhere in the chain of the development of the traditions also incorporated in the Damascus Document and the Community Rule.

The relationship between 4Q265 on the one hand, and S and D on the other hand is frequently described in terms of a 'hybrid' (Vermes 1997: 153), a 'medley' (Wise, Abegg, and Cook 1996: 278), or a 'combination' (García Martínez 1998: 214). This language goes back partly to Milik. Milik employed the term hybrid in the context of his description of 4Q265 but not, to be precise, with reference to the literary make-up of 4Q265. Rather, Milik speaks of 4Q265 as reflecting a 'hybrid type of life', that is, a stage in the development of the community when married members were admitted into the fellowship alongside celibate ones (1959: 96). In the course of time, Milik's terminology for a stage in the development of the community came to be applied to the literary character of 4Q265. Methodologically there is always the danger of allowing the order in which pieces of the jigsaw reach the scholarly tables to influence one's reading and evaluation of the texts. Thus, although all the evidence has only become fully available in the course of the last few years, a large proportion of the Damascus Document and the Community Rule have long been known. It is, therefore, perhaps a tempting suggestion to argue that, since 4Q265 contains elements reminiscent of both D and S, it is made up of 'extracts' from the known works (Wise, Abegg, and Cook 1996: 278). This interpretation of the relationship may indeed be a possible one, but it is certainly no more than that. This possibility needs to be confirmed as plausible or even probable by carefully analysing the evidence and by being aware of and thinking through all other available explanations. As will emerge from the overview of the contents of 4Q265 presented below, a description of this text as comprising excerpts from D and S does not stand up to closer scrutiny. At the very least such a judgment is in need of some refinement.

10

PHYSICAL DESCRIPTION AND CONTENTS OF THE FRAGMENTS

Physical Description

4QMiscellaneous Rules comprises seven identified fragments (4Q265 1–7) and twelve unidentified fragments (4Q265 a–1). Most of the latter fragments are very small indeed, whereas some of the identified fragments are of good size. In what follows the references to 4Q265 are based on the recently published official edition in the DJD series (Baumgarten 1999). The script of 4Q265 has been dated to the Herodian period (c. 30–50 CE) (Milik 1959: 96).

Outline of the Contents

In what follows I will provide a brief outline of the contents of 4Q265. The arrangement of the fragments of 4Q265 in the recent DJD edition reflects significant changes in terms of the sequence and numbering of the preserved fragments (Baumgarten 1999). In what follows I have adopted the references from the DJD edition but left the sequence in which the fragments are discussed unchanged. Thus, what follows adheres to the sequence of fragments as reflected in discussions of this text that pre-date the official edition (e.g. Baumgarten 1998).

Remnants of Penal-Code Traditions
(4Q265 4 i 2–ii 2)
This sizeable block of material comprises remnants of a penal code reminiscent of the penal material preserved in the Damascus Document (cf. CD 14.18b-22; 4QD^a 10 i 11–ii 15; 4QD^b 9 vi 1-5; 4QD^d 11 i 1-8; ii 1-2; 4QD^e 7 i 1-15) and the Community Rule (cf. 1QS 6.24–7.25; 4QS^d

V.1; 4QS^c I.4-15; II.3-8; 4QS^g 3.2-4; 4a-b. 1-7; 5a-c. 1-9; 6a-e. 1-5). The references to 4QS here and elsewhere are based on the recent edition of these manuscripts by P.S. Alexander and G. Vermes (1998). A further fragment preserving penal code material from Cave 11 was recently published by García Martínez, Tigchelaar and van der Woude (1998: 433-34).

Although both formally and in terms of content this material is closely related to the penal codes known from the Community Rule and the Damascus Document, it simplifies matters unduly to speak of the version represented by 4Q265 as comprising an excerpt. Although 4Q265 is only fragmentarily preserved, it is clear that it contains a traditio-historically independent version of the penal code from those preserved in S and D. This can be illustrated by means of the penalties as well as one of the offences that represent an independent stage in the development of the penal code in 4Q265 (see the helpful table in Baumgarten 1992d: 275-76). As far as the penalties are concerned, the most remarkable difference in 4Q265 is the repeated imposition of a cut of the offender's food ration by half (e.g. 4Q265 4 i 5, 8, 10). A similar but less severe cut in the food rations by one quarter is stipulated once in the lengthy code preserved in S (1QS 6.25 par. 4QS^g 3.4). As far as the offences in 4Q265 are concerned, of which even less text has survived, it is nevertheless apparent that 4Q265 4 ii 1-2 preserves an independent development of the offence of falling asleep during a session of the many. This offence forms part of all three penal codes as known from S, D, and 4Q265, but only in 4Q265 4 ii 2 is it followed by a specification apparently referring to a reading that formed part of the session of the many. In sum, it seems clear that 4Q265 preserves an independent tradition of the penal code. A question that arises from the differences between 4Q265 and the other penal codes is which of them may represent an earlier or later version. Because of the extremely limited amount of text preserved in 4Q265 this question is difficult to answer with confidence. Baumgarten has ventured the suggestion that the very severe cuts in the food ration laid down in 4Q265 would inevitably have led to undernourishment and he, therefore, considers the less severe cut in 1QS to represent 'a lessening of the harsher penance previously imposed' (1992d: 274). García Martínez argues for the reverse and suggests that '4QSD knows both 4QD and 1QS and modifies them in the direction of a more lenient position' (1998: 215). He appears to follow Milik (1959: 96) and understand 1QS 6.25 to refer to a reduction to a quarter of one's food rather than a reduction by a quarter (García Martínez 1994: 10; but contrast García Martínez and Tigchelaar 1997: I, 85). It is also noteworthy how frequently the cut in food forms part of the penalties in the relatively small amount of text preserved in 4Q265 in contrast to 1QS where a similar penalty is found only once. Finally, it is worth mentioning that neither CD nor the additional penal code material contained in 4QD[a, b, d, e] make reference to such a punishment. This difference may indicate that the community behind the D penal code did not take their meals in common (cf. Baumgarten 1992d: 272; García Martínez 1998: 215).

On the Admission of New Members
(4Q265 4 ii 3-9)

The remainder of the second column of fragment 4 seems to preserve the fragmentary remains of a passage describing the examination of candidates for admission into the community. The new topic seems to begin in line 3, although because the beginning of the line is lost we do not know whether it was once introduced with an introductory statement.

As was the case with the penal-code material, legislation on the admission process is found both in the Damascus Document (CD 15.5b–16.6a; 4QD[a] 8 i 1-9; 4QD[e] 6 i 21; ii 5-10, 17-19 ; 4QD[f] 4 i 10-12; ii 1-7) and the Community Rule (1QS 5.7c-10a; 6.13b-23; 4QS[b] IX.6b-8a; XI, 8.11-13; 4QS[d] I.5b-7a; 4QS[g] 3.1). The fragmentary nature of the material in 4Q265 makes it difficult to establish the relationship of this material to S and D with confidence. However, a number of observations can nevertheless be made.

Both in terminology and procedure the fragmentary remains of 4Q265 are more closely related to the legislation in 1QS 6.13b-24 (cf. 4QS[b] XI.8, 11-13; 4QS[g] 3.1) than to the procedure as stipulated in the Damascus Document (see also García Martínez 1998: 214). This may be illustrated by means of the following list of correspondences: 'council of the community' (4Q265 4 ii 3; 1QS 6.14, 16), 'a (complete) year' (4Q265 4 ii 4; 1QS 6.17-18 par. 4QS[b] XI.13; CD 15.15), 'a further/second (complete) year' (4Q265 4 ii 7; 1QS 6.21); 'being questioned' (4Q265 4 ii 5; 1QS 6.18); 'insight' (4Q265 4 ii 4; 1QS 6.14, 18); 'the many' (4Q265 4 ii 4, 5, 8; 1QS 6.14, 15, 16, 17 [twice, once paralleled in 4QS[b] XI.12], 18, 20 [three occurrences], 21; CD 15.8); 'to examine' (4Q265 4 ii 4; 1QS 6.14, 17; CD 15.11). Thus, in terms of terminology we may summarize that although a number of terms and expressions occur in all three documents there is a significantly greater amount of terminological overlap between 4Q265 and 1QS 6 par. 4QS. Moreover, in 4Q265 and S the admission process appears to extend over *several* years, as indicated by the explicit reference to a further complete year in 4Q265 4 ii 7 or a second year according to 1QS 6.21 in contrast to CD 15–16. In spite of these correspondences between 4Q265 and 1QS 6 par., the former nevertheless appears to preserve an independent tradition of the admission legislation and cannot accurately be described as an 'extract' of the latter.

Citation of Isaiah 54.1-2
(4Q265 1.1-6)
The opening lines of this fragment contain the remains of two introductory formulae. Only the words 'which is written' are preserved in line
2. The second formula is more fully preserved and reads 'it is written in
the bo[ok of] Isaiah the prophet' (4Q265 1.3). This is followed by a
partially preserved citation of Isa. 54.1-2. Since the text breaks off in the
middle of Isa. 54.2 the context of this citation is entirely lost leaving us in
the dark as to the possible function it might have had in the text.

Citation of Malachi 2.10 and Restrictions on Eating the Passover Meal
(4Q265 3.1-3)
Here we have a citation from Mal. 2.10 followed by a prohibition on
young boys and women partaking of the Passover sacrifice. The requirements for celebrating Passover have undergone considerable development
as reflected in biblical and post-biblical sources. Whereas in Exodus 12 the
Passover is intrinsically connected with individual households, the book of
Deuteronomy famously transforms it into a festival to be observed at the
central sanctuary. Hand in hand with this development questions of ritual
purity began to arise (see Baumgarten 1998: 31). Thus, both the Temple
Scroll (11QT^a 17.8-9) and the book of *Jubilees* (*Jub.* 49.17) limit participation in the Passover meal to anyone who is at least 20 years old.
Although both of the latter passages are frequently interpreted as excluding
women alongside minors (see Baumgarten 1998: 21), 4Q265 is the only
witness to mention the case of women explicitly. Baumgarten has argued
that the citation of Mal. 2.10 can be related to the question of who may
eat the Passover sacrifice if we understand the allusion to faithlessness and
defilement in the biblical text to refer to the more lenient practice regarding
the Passover attested in Josephus (*War* 6.426) and the Mishnah (*m. Pes.*
8.1) according to which women who were in a state of ritual purity were
permitted to partake of the meal (see Baumgarten 1998: 31-32).

On Agriculture(?)
(4Q265 5.1-4)
Fragment 5 contains a small amount of text, and its contents can only be
described in tentative terms. The references in line 1 to 'things sown' and
in line 2 to 'causing to sprout' suggest the possibility of an agricultural
context (Baumgarten 1998: 25).

On the Sabbath
(4Q265 6.1–7.6)
Alongside the penal-code traditions preserved in fragment 4 this extensive

section on the sabbath forms one of the most substantially preserved portions of 4Q265. As we saw above, the topic of the sabbath is dealt with at great length in the Damascus Document (CD 10.14–11.18b; 4QD^a 9 i 1-4; 4QD^b 9 ii 2-3, 8; 4QD^e 6 v 1-21; 4QD^f 5 i 1-12), and the relationship of the sabbath material in 4Q265 to the comparable portion of the Damascus Document is a crux for understanding the relationship of both documents as well as the character of 4Q265 in particular. Scholarly study of these issues is still in its infancy.

The remains of eight prohibited activities are preserved in 4Q265. Some of these overlap with activities mentioned in the sabbath legislation known from the Damascus Document. Moreover, stylistically both texts correspond very closely. Apart from these similarities there are also significant differences to be noted.

1. There are a number of cases that appear in 4Q265 but are absent from D such as the fragmentary reference to a war scenario in 4Q265 6.8 and the prohibition on priests sprinkling (purifying waters) on the sabbath in 4Q265 7.3. The prohibition is, however, attested in the as yet only partially and preliminarily published halakhic text 4Q274 1 ii 2 (Baumgarten 1998: 26; now see also Baumgarten *et al.* 1999: 103-104). Similarly absent from the sabbath legislation in D is the reference to the Day of Atonement attested in 4Q265 7.4 as well as the stipulation of a distance of 30 *ris* from the temple in 4Q265 7.6. The former reference to the Day of Atonement in a section containing predominantly sabbath halakhah is unusual. Baumgarten has offered a discussion and suggestions for restoration (1998: 26-27). As far as the latter stipulation is concerned, Baumgarten has plausibly suggested that the context of the distance of 30 *ris* from the temple may form part of a prescription relating to non-sacral slaughter as laid down in the Temple Scroll (11QT^a 52.17-19) (Baumgarten 1998: 27). It is not clear whether such a prescription had a sabbath connection. Instead, it seems equally possible that it followed the sabbath limits for pasturing animals discussed in the previous line, because both prescriptions share the general topic of laying down rules of geographical distance. It seems as if the topic of the sabbath, although clearly the predominant subject of this section, has been interspersed with a number of diverse statements that may have been evoked by a detail in the sabbath halakhot. Because of the fragmentary nature of the preserved text these observations are inevitably tentative.

2. Even where the same overall topic is dealt with in 4Q265 and D, both the wording as well as the substance of a number of stipulations differ in both accounts. This is the case for the two prohibitions on wearing unsuitable clothes in 4Q265 6.2-3 which resemble CD 11.3, but each text continues very differently. Apart from some differences in the wording of

4Q265 6.4 and CD 11.7-8 the lengthy passage dealing with the saving of human life on the sabbath in 4Q265 6.6-8 is the most important witness to this. In contrast to the Damascus Document (CD 11.16-17 par. 4QDᵉ 6 v 19-20), 4Q265 introduces the possibility of making use of one's garment to rescue a human being from drowning. This material has recently been examined at some length by L. Döring (1997: 264-74).

These differences between the sabbath legislation as found in 4Q265 and the Damascus Document leave no doubt that 4Q265 preserves independent traditions of sabbath halakhah. As far as the particular issue of saving human life on the sabbath is concerned, Döring argues 'The instruction to employ a garment [...] represents a traditio-historically advanced, quite sophisticated stage in the development of this view' (1997: 267). Elsewhere he goes further to propose that 4Q265 represents a later stage in the development of the sabbath code as known from the Damascus Document that is intent on 'clarifying halakhic problems which still have been left open' (Döring 1997: 274). It remains to be seen whether further study will uphold this hypothesis.

On the Make-up and Purpose of the Council of the Community (4Q265 7.7-10)

This fragmentarily preserved passage describes the make-up and purpose of the council of the community, which is said to comprise 15 members. With reference to a closely related passage in the Community Rule (cf. 1QS 8.1-16a; 4QSᵈ VI.1-8a; 4QSᵉ II.9b-18; III.6a) it is disputed how to understand this fifteen-strong 'council of the community'. Some have argued that the passage in 1QS 8 is best taken to describe an inner council of community leaders (Baumgarten 1976; Milik 1959: 100). Others have emphasized that elsewhere in 1QS the same expression designates the whole community. Thus, in the legislation on the admission of new members in 1QS 6 the community is designated by the expression 'the council of the community' in 1QS 6.14, 16b. A number of scholars, therefore, prefer to take the references to the council of the community in 1QS 8 as applying to the whole community also. The small number of members is, furthermore, then explained by arguing that 1QS 8 describes the community before its inception as the repeated phrase 'when there will be' in 1QS 8.4, 12 (see also 4QSᵈ VI.6 and 4QSᵉ [II.13]; III.3) seems to indicate (Sutcliffe 1959, who is followed by a series of later commentators).

The new evidence of a closely related passage in 4Q265 is unlikely to bring this long-standing debate to a close. Rather, 4Q265 seems to present us with much the same situation as is reflected in the Community Rule. That is to say, the present passage deals with a council of the community comprising the relatively small number of 15 members, and its inception is referred to as a future event (4Q265 7.7). Moreover, elsewhere in 4Q265, namely in the context of the legislation on the admission of new members in 4Q265 4 ii 3-9, the expression 'council of the [communi]ty' occurs apparently with reference to the community as a whole. Rather than offering a solution to the debate on the meaning of the expression 'council of the community' that was raised by 1QS 8 and parallels, 4Q265 merely mirrors the evidence known from the Community Rule in all its complexity.

It seems more likely to me that the value of the new text will come to be seen to lie in the realm of illuminating the literary development of the tradition on this topic as preserved in S and 4Q265. The existence of a literary and traditio-historical relationship of some kind between 1QS 8.1-16a par. and this part of 4Q265 is indicated by an impressive number of correspondences between both texts:

1. Both 4Q265 7.7-8 and 1QS 8.5 par. 4QS^e II.13 share the subject matter of the council of the community.
2. Both texts specify the number 15 for the membership of the council of the community, cf. 1QS 8.1 par. 4QS^e II.9 (twelve lay members and three priests) and 4Q265 7.7 (fifte[en ?]—after which the text breaks off).
3. The characteristic Hebrew verb form 'when there will be/exist' that occurs with reference to the council as an entity of the future in 1QS 8.4-5, 12 par. 4QS^d VI.6 and 4QS^e [II.13]; III.3 is found also in 4Q265 7.7.
4. The idea of atonement for the land comes to the fore in 4Q265 7.9 as well as in 1QS 8.6 par. [4QS^e II.15] and the superlinear addition in 1QS 8.10 par. [4QS^d VI.4].
5. Both 4Q265 7.9 and 1QS 8.9 par. [4QS^d VI.3]; 4QS^e II.17 make reference to a soothing odour. The underlying idea that the new community serves as a substitute for the temple, which is explicit in 1QS 8 par., appears to be present in 4Q265 7.9 also.
6. A reference to injustice occurs in 4Q265 7.10 ('times of injustice') and in the superlinear addition in 1QS 8.10 par. [4QS^d VI.5] ('no more injustice').
7. The hope for an eschatological judgment of the wicked is expressed both in 1QS 8.10 (the superlinear addition which appears to have been present in 4QS^d VI but absent from 4QS^e II.18–III.1 [cf. Alexander and Vermes 1998: 145]) as well as in 4Q265 7.10.
8. Finally, something of a curiosity in 4Q265's description of the council of the community is the partially preserved but probable reference to the prophets in 4Q265 7.8. Since the context of the

occurrence of the term is damaged it is extremely difficult to establish its significance here (see Baumgarten 1998: 27). It is noteworthy, however, that a reference to the revelation received through the prophets occurs also in 1QS 8.16 par. [4QS^d VI.8].

Alongside this impressive list of correspondences, which makes it appear likely that a literary relationship of some kind exists between both compositions, a number of differences need to be noted. Although subject matter and terminology frequently overlap, 4Q265 does appear to preserve an independent version of this material. Telling examples are the expressions 'council of the community' and 'when there are/exist' which do occur in both documents, but the exact phrase found in 4Q265 7.7, 'when there are in the council of the community', never occurs in S. Further examples of this nature could be added to this.

In sum, although 4Q265 7.7-10 does not appear to be an extract from 1QS 8 par., the correspondences that we observed between both passages are remarkable and point in the direction of a direct or indirect literary relationship.

The Purity of the Garden of Eden and Purification after Childbirth (4Q265 7.11-17)

The beginning of line 11 has been left blank, which seems to indicate the beginning of a new topic at this point. The material in this section is closely related to *Jubilees* 3. The book of *Jubilees* offers a retelling of Genesis and parts of Exodus. A characteristic feature of the retelling of the biblical story in *Jubilees* is the way the author portrays the primeval and patriarchal periods as a time when the laws laid down in the rest of the Pentateuch were already being observed. In *Jubilees* 3 we are told that Adam and Eve did not enter the Garden of Eden until they had undergone a period of purification of different length (40 days in Adam's case and 80 days in the case of Eve) because of the holiness of the Garden. The length of the respective periods of purification is derived from the legislation on the purification after childbirth as laid down in Leviticus 12. Moreover, *Jub.* 3.10-11 explicitly refers to Leviticus 12 in this context. In a paper devoted to 4Q265 7.11-17, J.M. Baumgarten (1994) notes the close similarities between this text and *Jubilees* 3. Both passages explicitly refer to the halakhic requirements laid down in Lev. 12.1-5 which prohibit women from entering the sanctuary for 40 days after giving birth to a male child and 80 days after the birth of a female child. What is more, in both texts these periods of purification are applied to Adam's and Eve's entry into the Garden of Eden. As Baumgarten has pointed out, both *Jubilees* 3 and 4Q265 apparently perceive the Garden of Eden as 'a prototype of the sanctuary' (1994: 6).

The close relationship between this part of 4Q265 and the book of *Jubilees* sets apart the present passage from the remainder of 4Q265 to some degree. The topic of purification after childbirth is also dealt with in one of the Cave 4 manuscripts of the Damascus Document, cf. 4QD[a] 6 ii 5-13. This part of 4QD[a] is closely based on Leviticus 12, and in distinction from 4Q265 and *Jubilees* no connection is made with the primeval period. Thus, although the topic of purification after childbirth raised in 4Q265 is an issue dealt with also in the Damascus Document, the manner in which this halakhic issue is related to a narrative about the Garden of Eden brings the present passage much closer to the book of *Jubilees* than to either the Damascus Document or the Community Rule.

Small Fragments
(4Q265 2.1-3; 4Q265 4 i a; 4Q265 4 i b; 4Q265 5a; and the unidentified fragments 4Q265 a–1)
A number of poorly preserved smaller fragments have further been identified as belonging to this text. In the great majority of cases it is not possible to establish with any degree of confidence the topics dealt with in the sparse remains that have survived.

Further Reading

On the penal code
Baumgarten, J.M.
1992d   'The Cave 4 Versions of the Qumran Penal Code', *JJS* 43: 268-76.
García Martínez, F.
1998   'The History of the Qumran Community in the Light of Recently Available Texts', in F.H. Cryer and T.L. Thompson (eds.), *Qumran Between the Old and New Testaments* (Copenhagen International Seminar, 6; JSOTSup, 290; Sheffield: Sheffield Academic Press): 194-216, esp. 213-15.
García Martínez, F., E.J.C. Tigchelaar, and A.S. van der Woude
1998   *Qumran Cave 11. II. 11Q2–18, 11Q20–31* (DJD, 23; Oxford: Clarendon Press): 433-34.

On the admission process
García Martínez, F.
1998   'The History of the Qumran Community in the Light of Recently Available Texts', in F.H. Cryer and T.L. Thompson (eds.), *Qumran Between the Old and New Testaments* (Copenhagen International Seminar, 6; JSOTSup, 290; Sheffield: Sheffield Academic Press): 194-216, esp. 214.

On the sabbath halakhah
Baumgarten, J.M.
1998   'Scripture and Law in 4Q265', in M.E. Stone and E.G. Chazon (eds.), *Biblical Perspectives: Early Use and Interpretation of the Bible in Light of the Dead Sea Scrolls* (STDJ, 28; Leiden: E.J. Brill): 25-33.

Döring, L.
    1997   'New Aspects of Qumran Sabbath Law from Cave 4 Fragments', in M.
                Bernstein, F. García Martínez, and J. Kampen (eds.), *Legal Texts and Legal
                Issues: Proceedings of the Second Meeting of the International Organization for
                Qumran Studies, Published in Honour of Joseph M. Baumgarten* (STDJ, 23;
                Leiden: E.J. Brill): 251-74.
Schiffman, L.H.
    1994   *Reclaiming the Dead Sea Scrolls: The History of Judaism, the Background of
                Christianity, the Lost Library of Qumran* (Philadelphia: Jewish Publication
                Society of America): esp. 275-82.

On the council of the community

Baumgarten, J.M.
    1976   'The Duodecimal Courts of Qumran, Revelation, and the Sanhedrin', *JBL*
                95: 59-78.
Sutcliffe, E.F., SJ
    1959   'The First Fifteen Members of the Qumran Community: A Note on 1QS
                8:1 ff.', *JSS* 4: 134-38.

On the purity of Eden and purification after childbirth

Baumgarten, J.M.
    1994   'Purification after Childbirth and the Sacred Garden in 4Q265 and Jubilees',
                in G.J. Brooke with F. García Martínez (eds.), *New Qumran Texts and
                Studies: Proceedings of the First Meeting of the International Organization for
                Qumran Studies, Paris 1992* (STDJ, 15; Leiden: E.J. Brill): 3-10.

11

THE PLACE OF 4Q265 IN THE LIBRARY OF QUMRAN

As became clear in the previous chapter, the genre and form of 4Q265 are exceedingly difficult to determine because of its fragmentary nature. It further emerged that 4Q265 displays close similarities in subject matter and style to a number of other works that belong to the Qumran library. As a consequence, attempts at understanding the nature of this composition and its place at Qumran have thus far focused on examining its relationship to these other texts. The contents of 4Q265 are closely related to the legal part of D, the central part of S (1QS 6–8 par.), and *Jubilees* 3.

The fullest discussion to date of the genre of 4Q265 and its place at Qumran has been offered by its editor in a recent paper (Baumgarten 1998: 29). Baumgarten begins by drawing out the possible relevance of a category of biblical texts that has been characterized by E. Tov (1995) as 'Excerpted and Abbreviated Biblical Texts'. A difficulty with the frequently held 'excerpts-hypothesis', of which these observations represent a version, is that although the topics dealt with in 4Q265 overlap with S, D, and *Jubilees*, the material in 4Q265 frequently represents an independent treatment of these overlapping topics. In recent years it has become increasingly apparent that both S and D are the products of a complex history of composition and redaction. The relationship between 4Q265 on the one hand and S and D on the other hand seems to me to pre-date the final forms of D and S as they are represented by the texts available to us. These observations indicate that although 4Q265 may well contain excerpts of some kind, it is by no means clear from what kind of work or works the excerpts were taken. In any case, its relationship to D and S has emerged as far more complex than that of a work of excerpts to the sources from which the excerpts have been extracted. Let me take the sabbath legislation as an example. It seems very likely that 4Q265 represents a development of sabbath-code traditions of the kind contained within the Laws of D. It is not at all self-evident, however, that the compiler or author of 4Q265 drew on a sabbath code that was already part of a larger document such as the Damascus Document in its present form.

In addition to drawing on the partial analogy of excerpted and abbreviated biblical texts, Baumgarten further emphasizes the formal resemblance between 4Q265 and 4QOrdinances[a] (4Q159). In particular, he stresses the presence of halakhic material alongside some narrative sections in both works as well as the variety of the material preserved in both texts (1998: 29-30).

The debate on the genre and place of 4Q265 in the Qumran collection has just begun and is likely to exercise scholars for the foreseeable future. Although no conclusive results have been arrived at as yet, it seems clear that the relationship between 4Q265 and other closely related compositions emerges as a rather more complex one than earlier preliminary descriptions of the work as containing excerpts from S and D may have led us to imagine. It seems appropriate to end with some apposite words by the editor of this text, who concludes a recent study with the observation that 4Q265 is 'a most interesting specimen of an eclectic Qumran text, for which the provisional designation Serek-Dameseq no longer seems adequate' (Baumgarten 1998: 33).

Further Reading

Baumgarten, J.M.
    1998   'Scripture and Law in 4Q265', in M.E. Stone and E.G. Chazon (eds.), *Biblical Perspectives: Early Use and Interpretation of the Bible in Light of the Dead Sea Scrolls* (STDJ, 28; Leiden: E.J. Brill): 25-33.

Bibliography

Printed resources

Albani, M.
    1997   'Zur Rekonstruktion eines verdrängten Konzepts: Der 364-Tage-Kalender in der gegenwärtigen Forschung', in M. Albani, J. Frey, and A. Lange (eds.), *Studies in the Book of Jubilees* (Texte und Studien zum Antiken Judentum, 65; Tübingen: Mohr Siebeck): 79-125.

Albright, W.F., and C.S. Mann
    1969   'Qumran and the Essenes: Geography, Chronology, and Identification of the Sect', in Black 1969: 11-25.

Alexander, P.S., and G. Vermes
    1998   *Qumran Cave 4. XIX. Serekh ha-Yaḥad and Two Related Texts* (DJD, 26; Oxford: Clarendon).

Baillet, M., J.T. Milik, and R. de Vaux, OP
    1962   *Les 'Petites Grottes' de Qumrân: Exploration de la falaise, les grottes 2Q, 3Q, 5Q, 6Q, 7Q à 10Q, le rouleau de cuivre* (DJD, 3; Oxford: Clarendon).

Baltzer, K.
    1971   *The Covenant Formulary in Old Testament, Jewish, and Early Christian Writings* (ET, D.E. Green; Oxford: Blackwell).

Bardtke, H.
    1961   *Die Handschriftenfunde am Toten Meer: Die Sekte von Qumran* (Berlin: Evangelische Haupt-Bibelgesellschaft, 2nd edn).

Baumgarten, J.M.
    1967   'The Essene Avoidance of Oil and the Laws of Purity', *RevQ* 6: 183-92.
    1976   'The Duodecimal Courts of Qumran, Revelation, and the Sanhedrin', *JBL* 95: 59-78.
    1987   'The Laws of ᶜOrlah and First Fruits in the Light of Jubilees, the Qumran Writings, and Targum Ps. Jonathan', *JJS* 38: 195-202.
    1990   'The 4Q Zadokite Fragments on Skin Disease', *JJS* 41: 153-65.
    1992a   'A New Qumran Substitute for the Divine Name and Mishnah Sukkah 4.5', *JQR* 83: 1-5.
    1992b   'The Disqualifications of Priests in 4Q Fragments of the "Damascus Document": A Specimen of the Recovery of pre-Rabbinic Halakha', in Trebolle Barrera and Vegas Montaner 1992: II, 503-13.
    1992c   'A "Scriptural" Citation in 4Q Fragments of the Damascus Document', *JJS* 43: 95-98.
    1992d   'The Cave 4 Versions of the Qumran Penal Code', *JJS* 43: 268-76.
    1992e   'The Laws of the Damascus Document in Current Research', in Broshi 1992: 51-62.
    1994   'Purification after Childbirth and the Sacred Garden in 4Q265 and Jubilees', in G.J. Brooke with F. García Martínez (eds.), *New Qumran Texts and Studies: Proceedings of the First Meeting of the International Organization for Qumran Studies, Paris 1992* (STDJ, 15; Leiden: E.J. Brill): 3-10.

1995   'A Qumran Text with Agrarian Halakhah', *JQR* 86: 1-8.
1996   *Qumran Cave 4*. XIII. *The Damascus Document (4Q266-273)* (DJD, 18; Oxford: Clarendon).
1998   'Scripture and Law in 4Q265', in M.E. Stone and E.G. Chazon (eds.), *Biblical Perspectives: Early Use and Interpretation of the Bible in Light of the Dead Sea Scrolls* (STDJ, 28; Leiden: E.J. Brill): 25-33.
2000   'The Laws of the Damascus Document: Between the Bible and the Mishnah', in Baumgarten, Chazon, and Pinnick 2000: 17-26.

Baumgarten, J.M., E. Chazon, and A. Pinnick (eds.)
2000   *The Damascus Document: A Centennial of Discovery. Proceedings of the Third International Symposium of the Orion Center* (STDJ, 34; Leiden: E.J. Brill).

Baumgarten, J.M., with M.T. Davis
1995   'Cave IV, V, VI Fragments Related to the Damascus Document (4Q266-273 = 4QD^{a-h}, 5Q12 = 5QD, 6Q15 = 6QD', in Charlesworth *et al.* 1995: 59-79.

Baumgarten, J.M., and D.R. Schwartz, with an appendix by Y. Ofer
1995   'The Damascus Document (CD)', in Charlesworth 1995: 4-57.

Baumgarten, J.M., *et al.*
1999   *Qumran Cave 4*. XXV. *Halakhic Texts* (DJD, 35; Oxford: Clarendon Press).

Beall, T.S.
1988   *Josephus' Description of the Essenes Illustrated by the Dead Sea Scrolls* (SNTSMS, 58; Cambridge: Cambridge University Press).

Bergmeier, R.
1993   *Die Essener-Berichte des Flavius Josephus: Quellenstudien zu den Essenertexten im Werk des Jüdischen Historiographen* (Kampen: Kok Pharos).

Bernstein, M.J., F. García Martínez, and J. Kampen (eds.)
1997   *Legal Texts and Legal Issues: Proceedings of the Second Meeting of the International Organization for Qumran Studies, Published in Honour of Joseph M. Baumgarten* (STDJ, 23; Leiden: E.J. Brill).

Bilde, P.
1998   'The Essenes in Philo and Josephus', in Cryer and Thompson 1998: 32-68.

Black, M. (ed.)
1969   *The Scrolls and Christianity: Historical and Theological Significance* (London: SPCK).

Boyce, M.
1988   'The Poetry of the Damascus Document' (University of Edinburgh: PhD Thesis).
1990   'The Poetry of the *Damascus Document* and its Bearing on the Origin of the Qumran Sect', *RevQ* 14: 615-28.

Brin, G.
1997   'Divorce at Qumran', in Bernstein, García Martínez, and Kampen 1997: 231-44.

Brooke, G.J.
1980   'The Amos–Numbers Midrash (CD 7 13b–8 1a) and Messianic Expectation', *ZAW* 92: 397-404.
1991   'The Messiah of Aaron in the Damascus Document', *RevQ* 15: 215-30.

Broshi, M. (ed.)
1992   *The Damascus Document Reconsidered* (Jerusalem: Israel Exploration Society, The Shrine of the Book, Israel Museum).

Burchard, C.
1957   *Bibliographie zu den Handschriften vom Toten Meer* (BZAW, 76; Berlin: Töpelmann).

1965   *Bibliographie zu den Handschriften vom Toten Meer*. II. *Nr. 1557-4459*
             (BZAW, 89; Berlin: Töpelmann).

Burrows, M.
1956   *The Dead Sea Scrolls* (London: Secker & Warburg).

Callaway, P.R.
1988   *The History of the Qumran Community: An Investigation* (JSOTSup, 3; Shef-
             field: JSOT Press).

Campbell, J.G.
1995   *The Use of Scripture in the Damascus Document* (BZAW, 228; Berlin: de
             Gruyter).

Carmignac, J.
1959   'Comparaison entre les manuscrits "A" et "B" du Document de Damas',
             RevQ 2: 53-67.

Charles, R.H.
1977 (1913)   *The Apocrypha and Pseudepigrapha of the Old Testament in English with
             Introductions and Critical and Explanatory Notes to the Several Books* (2 vols.;
             Oxford: Clarendon Press).

Charlesworth, J.H.
1980   'The Origin and Subsequent History of the Authors of the Dead Sea Scrolls:
             Four Transitional Phases Among the Qumran Essenes', *RevQ* 10: 213-33.

Charlesworth, J.H., with J.M. Baumgarten *et al.* (eds.)
1995   *The Dead Sea Scrolls: Hebrew, Aramaic, and Greek Texts with English Trans-
             lations. Damascus Document, War Scroll, and Related Documents* (The Prince-
             ton Theological Seminary Dead Sea Scrolls Project, 2; Tübingen: J.C.B.
             Mohr [Paul Siebeck]; Louisville, KY: Westminster/John Knox Press).

Collins, J.J.
1989   'The Origin of the Qumran Community: A Review of the Evidence', in
             M.P. Horgan and P.J. Kobelski (eds.), *To Touch the Text: Biblical and Re-
             lated Studies in Honor of Joseph A. Fitzmyer* (New York: Crossroad): 159-78.

1995   *The Scepter and the Star: The Messiahs of the Dead Sea Scrolls and Other
             Ancient Literature* (New York: Doubleday).

1997   *Apocalypticism in the Dead Sea Scrolls* (The Literature of the Dead Sea
             Scrolls; London: Routledge).

Cothenet, É.
1963   'Le Document de Damas', in J. Carmignac, É. Cothenet and H. Lignée
             (eds.), *Les textes de Qumran: traduits et annotés* (2 vols; Paris: Letouzey et
             Ané, 2nd edn): II, 149-204.

Cross, F.M.
1995   *The Ancient Library of Qumran* (The Biblical Seminar, 30; Sheffield: Shef-
             field Academic Press, rev. 3rd edn).

Cryer, F.H., and T.L. Thompson (eds.).
1998   *Qumran Between the Old and New Testaments* (Copenhagen International
             Seminar, 6; JSOTSup, 290; Sheffield: Sheffield Academic Press).

Davies, P.R.
1977   'Hasidim in the Maccabean Period', *JJS* 28: 127-40.
1983   *The Damascus Covenant: An Interpretation of the 'Damascus Document'*
             (JSOTSup, 25; Sheffield: Sheffield Academic Press).
1987   *Behind the Essenes: History and Ideology in the Dead Sea Scrolls* (BJS, 94;
             Atlanta: Scholars Press).
1988a   'The Teacher of Righteousness and the "End of Days" ', *RevQ* 13: 313-17.
1988b   'How Not to Do Archaeology: The Story of Qumran', *BA* 51: 203-207.
1990   'The Birthplace of the Essenes: Where is "Damascus"?', *RevQ* 14: 503-19.

1996		'Sadducees in the Dead Sea Scrolls', in *idem, Sects and Scrolls: Essays on Qum-ran and Related Topics* (South Florida Studies in the History of Judaism, 134; Atlanta: Scholars Press): 127-38.

Davis, R.
1992		'The History of the Composition of the Damascus Document Statutes (CD 9-16 + 4QD)' (University of Harvard: PhD dissertation).

Denis, A.-M.
1965		'Évolution de structures dans la secte de Qumrân', in J. Giblet *et al.* (eds.), *Aux origines de l'église* (Rech Bib, 7; Louvain: Desclée de Brouwer): 23-49.
1967		*Les thèmes de connaissance dans le Document de Damas* (Louvain: Publications Universitaires).

Dimant, D.
1984		'Qumran Sectarian Literature', in M.E. Stone (ed.), *Jewish Writings of the Second Temple Period: Apocrypha, Pseudepigrapha, Qumran Sectarian Writ-ings, Philo, Josephus* (CRINT, 2.II; Philadelphia: Fortress Press; Assen: Van Gorcum): 483-550.

Döring, L.
1997		'New Aspects of Qumran Sabbath Law from Cave 4 Fragments', in Bern-stein, García Martínez, and Kampen 1997: 251-74.

Duhaime, J.
1987		'Dualistic Reworking in the Scrolls from Qumran', *CBQ* 49: 32-56.

Dupont-Sommer, A.
1961		*The Essene Writings from Qumran* (ET, G. Vermes; Oxford: Blackwell).

Eshel, E.
1994		'4Q477: The Rebukes by the Overseer', *JJS* 45: 111-22.

Fitzmyer, J.A., SJ
1970		Prolegomenon to the reprint of S. Schechter, *Documents of Jewish Sectaries*. I. *Fragments of a Zadokite Work* (New York: Ktav): 9-37.
1990		*The Dead Sea Scrolls: Major Publications and Tools for Study* (SBLRBS, 20; Atlanta: Scholars Press, rev. edn).
1995		'The Qumran Community: Essene or Sadducean?', *HeyJ* 36: 467-76.
2000		'The Gathering in of the Teacher of the Community', in *idem, The Dead Sea Scrolls and Christian Origins* (Studies in the Dead Sea Scrolls and Related Literature; Grand Rapids: Eerdmans): 261-65.

Flint, P.W., and J.C. VanderKam (eds.)
1998		*The Dead Sea Scrolls after Fifty Years: A Comprehensive Assessment* (2 vols; Leiden: E.J. Brill): I.
1999		*The Dead Sea Scrolls after Fifty Years: A Comprehensive Assessment* (2 vols; Leiden: E.J. Brill): II.

García Martínez, F.
1988		'Qumran Origins and Early History: A Groningen Hypothesis', *Folia Orientalia* 25: 113-36.
1992		'Damascus Document: A Bibliography of Studies 1970–1989', in Broshi 1992: 63-83.
1994		*The Dead Sea Scrolls Translated: The Qumran Texts in English* (ET, W.G.E. Watson; Leiden: E.J. Brill).
1998		'The History of the Qumran Community in the Light of Recently Available Texts', in Cryer and Thompson 1998: 194-216.

García Martínez, F., and D.W. Parry
1996		*Bibliography of the Finds in the Desert of Judah 1970-1995* (STDJ, 19; Leiden: E.J. Brill).

García Martínez, F., and E.J.C. Tigchelaar
    1998   'Bibliography of the Dead Sea Scrolls', *RevQ* 18: 459-90, 605-39.
García Martínez, F., and E.J.C. Tigchelaar (eds.)
    1997   *The Dead Sea Scrolls Study Edition* (2 vols.; Leiden: E.J. Brill): I.
    1998   *The Dead Sea Scrolls Study Edition* (2 vols.; Leiden: E.J. Brill): II.
García Martínez, F., E.J.C. Tigchelaar, and A.S. van der Woude
    1998   *Qumran Cave 11. II. 11Q2–18, 11Q20–31* (DJD, 23; Oxford: Clarendon Press).
García Martínez, F., and J. Trebolle Barrera
    1995   *The People of the Dead Sea Scrolls: Their Writings, Beliefs and Practices* (Leiden: E.J. Brill).
Gaster, T.H.
    1957   *The Scriptures of the Dead Sea Sect in English Translation* (London: Secker & Warburg).
Ginzberg, L.
    1976 (1922)   *An Unknown Jewish Sect* (New York: Jewish Theological Seminary of America).
Glessmer, U.
    1999   'Calendars in the Dead Sea Scrolls', in Flint and VanderKam 1999: II, 213-78.
Goodman, M.D.
    1995   'A Note on the Qumran Sectarians, the Essenes and Josephus', *JJS* 46: 161-66.
Hayes, J.H., and J.M. Miller (eds.)
    1977   *Israelite and Judaean History* (London: SCM Press).
Hempel, C.
    1995   'Who Rebukes in 4Q477?', *RevQ* 16: 655-56.
    1997   'The Penal Code Reconsidered', in Bernstein, García Martínez, and Kampen 1997: 337-48.
    1998   *The Laws of the Damascus Document: Sources, Traditions and Redaction* (STDJ, 29; Leiden: E.J. Brill).
    1999   'Community Origins in the Damascus Document in the Light of Recent Scholarship', in D.W. Parry and E.C. Ulrich (eds.), *The Provo International Conference on the Dead Sea Scrolls: Technological Innovations, New Texts, and Reformulated Issues* (STDJ, 30; Leiden: E.J. Brill): 316-29.
    2000   'The Laws of the Damascus Document and 4QMMT', in Baumgarten, Chazon, and Pinnick 2000: 69-84.
Hengel, M.
    1981   *Judaism and Hellenism: Studies in their Encounter in Palestine during the Early Hellenistic Period* (London: SCM Press).
Instone Brewer, D.
    1998   'Nomological Exegesis in Qumran "Divorce" Texts', *RevQ* 18: 561-79.
Iwry, S.
    1969   'Was There a Migration to Damascus? The Problem of שבי ישראל', *Eretz Israel* 9: 80-88.
Jaubert, A.
    1958   'Le pays de Damas', *RB* 65: 214-48.
Jeremias, G.
    1963   *Der Lehrer der Gerechtigkeit* (SUNT, 2; Göttingen: Vandenhoeck & Ruprecht).

Jongeling, B.
　　1971　　*A Classified Bibliography of the Finds in the Desert of Judah 1958–1969* (STDJ, 7; Leiden: E.J. Brill).

Jull, A.T.T., D.J. Donahue, M. Broshi, and E. Tov
　　1996　　'Radiocarbon Dating of Scrolls and Linen Fragments from the Judean Desert', ᶜ*Atiqot* 28: 1-7.

Kahle, P.
　　1959　　*The Cairo Genizah* (Oxford: Blackwell, 2nd edn).

Kapelrud, A.S.
　　1968　　'Der Bund in den Qumran-Schriften', in S. Wagner (ed.), *Bibel und Qumran: Beiträge zur Erforschung der Beziehungen zwischen Bibel- und Qumranwissenschaft* (Berlin: Evangelische Haupt-Bibelgesellschaft): 137-49.

Knibb, M.A.
　　1976　　'The Exile in the Literature of the Intertestamental Period', *HeyJ* 17: 249-72.
　　1979　　'The Dead Sea Scrolls: Reflections on some Recent Publications', *Expository Times* 90: 294-300.
　　1983　　'Exile in the Damascus Document', *JSOT* 25: 99-117.
　　1987　　*The Qumran Community* (Cambridge Commentaries on Writings of the Jewish and Christian World 200 BC to AD 200; Cambridge: Cambridge University Press).
　　1989　　*Jubilees and the Origins of the Qumran Community: An Inaugural Lecture* (London: King's College).
　　1990　　'The Teacher of Righteousness—A Messianic Title?', in P.R. Davies and R.T. White (eds.), *A Tribute to Geza Vermes: Essays on Jewish and Christian Literature and History* (JSOTSup, 100; Sheffield: JSOT Press): 51-65.
　　1991　　'The Interpretation of Damascus Document VII, 9b-VIII, 2a and XIX, 5b-14', *RevQ* 15: 243-51.
　　1994　　'The Place of the Damascus Document', in M.O. Wise, N. Golb, J.J. Collins and D.G. Pardee (eds.), *Methods of Investigation of the Dead Sea Scrolls and the Khirbet Qumran Site: Present Realities and Future Prospects* (ANYAS, 722; New York: New York Academy of Sciences): 149-62.

Kuhn, K.G.
　　1959　　'The Two Messiahs of Aaron and Israel', in K. Stendahl (ed.), *The Scrolls and the New Testament* (London: SCM Press): 54-64.

Laato, A.
　　1992　　'The Chronology in the *Damascus Document* of Qumran', *RevQ* 15: 607-609.

Lagrange, M.-J.
　　1912　　'La secte juive de la Nouvelle Alliance au pays de Damas', *RB* NS 9: 213-40.

Laperrousaz, E.-M.
　　1976　　*Qoumrân: L'établissement essénien des bords de la Mer Morte. Histoire et archéologie du site* (Paris: A. & J. Picard).

LaSor, W.S.
　　1958　　*Bibliography of the Dead Sea Scrolls 1948–1957* (Fuller Library Bulletin, 31; Pasadena, CA: Fuller Theological Seminary Library).

Lévi, I.
　　1911–12　　'Un écrit sadducéen antérieur à la destruction du Temple', *REJ* 61: 161-205; 63: 1-19.
　　1913　　'Document relatif à la 'Communauté des fils de Sadoc'', *REJ* 65: 24-31.

Lohse, E.
　　1986　　*Die Texte aus Qumran* (Darmstadt: Wissenschaftliche Buchgesellschaft, 4th edn).

Magness, J.
1998   'Qumran Archaeology: Past Perspectives and Future Prospects', in Flint and
            VanderKam 1998: I, 47-77.
Maier, J.
1995   *Die Qumran-Essener: Die Texte vom Toten Meer* (UTB, 1862; 3 vols.; Basel:
            Friedrich Reinhardt): I.
1996a   *Die Qumran-Essener: Die Texte vom Toten Meer* (UTB, 1863; 3 vols.; Basel:
            Friedrich Reinhardt): II.
1996b   *Die Qumran-Essener: Die Texte vom Toten Meer* (UTB, 1916; 3 vols.; Basel:
            Friedrich Reinhardt): III.
Metso, S.
1997   *The Textual Development of the Qumran Community Rule* (STDJ, 21; Leiden:
            E.J. Brill).
Milik, J.T.
1959   *Ten Years of Discovery in the Wilderness of Judaea* (ET, J. Strugnell; London:
            SCM Press).
1966   'Fragment d'une source du Psautier (4QPs 89) et fragments des Jubilés, du
            Document de Damas, d'un Phylactère dans la Grotte 4 de Qumran', *RB* 73:
            94-106.
1972   'Milkî-ṣedeq et Milkî-rešaᶜ dans les anciens écrits juifs et chrétiens', *JJS* 23:
            95-144.
1977   'Numérotation des feuilles des rouleaux dans le scriptorium de Qmrân',
            Semitica 27: 75-81.
Milik, J.T. *et al.*
1956   'Le travail d'édition des fragments manuscrits de Qumrân', *RB* 63: 49-67.
Milikowsky, C.
1982   'Again: *Damascus* in Damascus Document and Rabbinic Literature', *RevQ*
            11: 97-106.
Murphy-O'Connor, J.
1970   'An Essene Missionary Document? CD II, 14–VI, 1', *RB* 77: 201-29.
1971a   'A Literary Analysis of Damascus Document VI, 2–VIII, 3', *RB* 78: 210-32.
1971b   'The Original Text of CD 7:9–8:2 = 19:5-14', *HTR* 64: 379-86.
1972a   'The Critique of the Princes of Judah (CD VIII, 3-19)', *RB* 79: 200-16.
1972b   'A Literary Analysis of Damascus Document XIX, 33–XX, 34', *RB* 79: 544-
            64.
1974   'The Essenes and their History', *RB* 81: 215-44.
1985   'The *Damascus Document* Revisited', *RB* 92: 223-46.
Nickelsburg, G.W.
1986   '*1 Enoch* and Qumran Origins: The State of the Question and Some
            Prospects for Answers', in K.H. Richards (ed.), *Society of Biblical Literature
            Seminar Papers* (Atlanta: Scholars Press): 341-60.
North, R.
1955   'The Damascus of Qumran Geography', *PEQ* 87: 34-48.
Qimron, E.
1991   'Notes on the 4Q Zadokite Fragments on Skin Disease', *JJS* 42: 256-59.
1992   'The Text of CDC', in Broshi 1992: 9-49.
Rabin, C.
1954   *The Zadokite Documents*. I. *The Admonition*. II. *The Laws* (Oxford: Claren-
            don).
1957   *Qumran Studies* (Oxford: Oxford University Press).
1958   *The Zadokite Documents*. I. *The Admonition*. II. *The Laws* (Oxford: Claren-
            don, rev. 2nd edn).

Rabinowitz, I.
   1954   'A Reconsideration of "Damascus" and "390 Years" in the "Damascus"
             ("Zadokite") Fragments', *JBL* 73: 11-35.
Reed, S.A.
   1996   'Genre, Setting and Title of 4Q477', *JJS* 47: 147-48.
Reif, S.
   2000   'Cairo Genizah', in L.H. Schiffman and J.C. VanderKam (eds.), *Ency-
             clopedia of the Dead Sea Scrolls* (2 vols.; New York: Oxford University Press):
             I, 105-108.
Rost, L.
   1933   *Die Damaskusschrift* (Kleine Texte für Vorlesungen und Übungen, 167;
             Berlin: de Gruyter).
Rowley, H.H.
   1952   *The Zadokite Fragments and the Dead Sea Scrolls* (Oxford: Blackwell).
Rubinstein, A.
   1952   'Urban Halakhah and Camp Rules in the "Cairo Fragments of a Damascene
             Covenant" ', *Sefarad* 12: 283-96.
Schechter, S.
   1910   *Documents of Jewish Sectaries*. I. *Fragments of a Zadokite Work* (Cambridge:
             Cambridge University Press).
Schiffman, L.H.
   1975   *The Halakha at Qumran* (SJLA, 16; Leiden: E.J. Brill).
   1983a   *Sectarian Law in the Dead Sea Scrolls: Courts, Testimony and the Penal Code*
             (BJS, 33; Chico, CA: Scholars Press).
   1983b   'Legislation Concerning Relations with Non-Jews in the *Zadokite Fragments*
             and in Tannaitic Literature', *RevQ* 11: 379-89.
   1990   'The New Halakhic Letter (4QMMT) and the Origins of the Dead Sea
             Sect', *BA* 53: 64-73.
   1993   'The Sadducean Origins of the Dead Sea Scroll Sect', in Shanks 1993: 35-
             49.
   1994   *Reclaiming the Dead Sea Scrolls: The History of Judaism, the Background of
             Christianity, the Lost Library of Qumran* (Philadelphia: Jewish Publication
             Society of America).
Schürer, E., G. Vermes, F. Millar, and M. Black
   1979   *The History of the Jewish People in the Age of Jesus Christ* (3 vols.; Edinburgh:
             T. & T. Clark): II.
Schwarz, O.J.R.
   1965   *Der erste Teil der Damaskusschrift und das Alte Testament* (Diest: Lichtland).
Shanks, H. (ed.)
   1993   *Understanding the Dead Sea Scrolls* (London: SPCK).
Soloff, R.A.
   1958   'Towards Uncovering Original Texts in the Zadokite Documents', *NTS* 5:
             62-67.
Stegemann, H.
   1971   *Die Entstehung der Qumrangemeinde* (Bonn: privately published).
   1990   'Das Gesetzeskorpus der "Damaskusschrift" (CD IX–XVI)', *RevQ* 14: 409-
             34.
   1992   'The Qumran Essenes—Local Members of the Main Jewish Union in Late
             Second Temple Times', in Trebolle Barrera and Vegas Montaner 1992: I,
             83-166.
   1998a   *The Library of Qumran: On the Essenes, Qumran, John the Baptist, and Jesus*
             (Grand Rapids: Eerdmans; Leiden: E.J. Brill).

1998b	'More Identified Fragments of *4QD^d* (*4Q269*)', *RevQ* 18: 497-509.
2000	'Towards Physical Reconstructions of the Qumran Damascus Document Scrolls', in Baumgarten, Chazon, and Pinnick 2000: 177-200.

Stemberger, G.
1995	*Jewish Contemporaries of Jesus: Pharisees, Sadducees, Essenes* (Minneapolis: Fortress Press).

Steudel, A.
1997	Review of E. Ulrich and J. VanderKam (eds.), *The Community of the Renewed Covenant*, in *RevQ* 18: 156-60.

Stone, M.E.
1991	'Enoch, Aramaic Levi and Sectarian Origins', in *idem, Selected Studies in Pseudepigrapha and Apocrypha: With Special Reference to the Armenian Tradition* (SVTP, 9; Leiden: E.J. Brill): 247-58.

Strickert, F.
1986	'Damascus Document VII, 10-20 and Qumran Messianic Expectation', *RevQ* 12: 327-49.

Sukenik, E.L.
1948	*Megillot genuzot mi-tokh genizah qedumah she-nimṣe'ah be-midbar Yehudah [Hidden Scrolls from the Ancient Genizah found in the Judaean Desert]* (Jerusalem: Bialik Institute).

Sutcliffe, E.F., SJ
1959	'The First Fifteen Members of the Qumran Community: A Note on 1QS 8:1 ff.', *JSS* 4: 134-38.
1960	*The Monks of Qumran: The People of the Dead Sea Scrolls* (London: Burns & Oates).

Talmon, S.
1965	'The Calendar Reckoning of the Sect from the Judaean Desert', in C. Rabin and Y. Yadin (eds.), *Scripta Hierosolymitana: Publications of the Hebrew University, Jerusalem.* VI. *Aspects of the Dead Sea Scrolls* (Jerusalem: Magnes Press): 162-99.
1989	*The World of Qumran from Within: Collected Studies* (Jerusalem: Magnes Press).
1994	'Qumran Studies: Past, Present, and Future', *JQR* 85: 1-31.

Tigay, J.H.
1993	'Examination of the Accused Bride in 4Q159: Forensic Medicine at Qumran', *JANES* 22: 129-34.

Tigchelaar, E.J.C.
1999	'More Identifications of Scraps and Overlaps', *RevQ* 19: 61-68.

Tiller, P.
1987	'The Laws of the Damascus Document and Qumran', *HNTSP* 1987 (unpublished).

Tov, E.
1995	'Excerpted and Abbreviated Biblical Texts from Qumran', *RevQ* 16: 581-600.

Tov, E., with the collaboration of S. Pfann (ed.)
1993	*The Dead Sea Scrolls on Microfiche: A Comprehensive Facsimile Edition of the Texts from the Judean Desert* (Leiden: E.J. Brill).

Trebolle Barrera, J., and L. Vegas Montaner (eds.)
1992	*The Madrid Qumran Congress: Proceedings of the International Congress on the Dead Sea Scrolls, Madrid 18–21 March 1991* (STDJ, 11; 2 vols.; Leiden: E.J. Brill).

VanderKam, J.C.

1992 'Calendars: Ancient Israelite and Early Jewish', in *Anchor Bible Dictionary* (6 vols; New York: Doubleday): I, 814-20.

1993 'The People of the Dead Sea Scrolls: Essenes or Sadducees?', in Shanks 1993: 50-62.

1994a *The Dead Sea Scrolls Today* (London: SPCK).

1994b 'Messianism in the Scrolls', in E. Ulrich and J.C. VanderKam (eds.), *The Community of the Renewed Covenant: The Notre Dame Symposium on the Dead Sea Scrolls* (Notre Dame: Notre Dame University Press): 211-34.

1998 *Calendars in the Dead Sea Scrolls: Measuring Time* (The Literature of the Dead Sea Scrolls; London: Routledge).

1999 'Identity and History of the Community', in Flint and VanderKam 1999: II, 487-533.

de Vaux, R.

1973 *Archaeology and the Dead Sea Scrolls* (London: Oxford University Press).

de Vaux, R., and J.T. Milik with contributions by J.W.B. Barns and J. Carswell

1977 *Qumrân Grotte 4*. II (DJD, 6; Oxford: Clarendon).

Vermes, G.

1973 *Scripture and Tradition in Judaism: Haggadic Studies* (Studia Post-Biblica, 4; Leiden: E.J. Brill).

1974 'Sectarian Matrimonial Halakhah in the Damascus Rule', *JJS* 25: 197-202.

1981 'The Essenes and History', *JJS* 32: 18-31.

1994 *The Dead Sea Scrolls: Qumran in Perspective* (London: SCM Press, rev. 3rd edn).

1997 *The Complete Dead Sea Scrolls in English* (London: Penguin Books).

Vermes, G., and M.D. Goodman

1989 *The Essenes: According to the Classical Sources* (Oxford Centre Textbooks, 1; Sheffield: JSOT Press).

Wacholder, B.Z.

1988 'Does Qumran Record the Death of the *Moreh*? The Meaning of *he'aseph* in *Damascus Covenant* XIX, 35, XX, 14', *RevQ* 13: 323-30.

Wacholder, B.Z., and M.G. Abegg on the basis of the transcriptions of J.T. Milik *et al*. (eds.)

1991 *A Preliminary Edition of the Unpublished Dead Sea Scrolls: The Hebrew and Aramaic Texts from Cave Four* (4 fascicles; Washington DC: Biblical Archaeology Society): I.

1995 *A Preliminary Edition of the Unpublished Dead Sea Scrolls: The Hebrew and Aramaic Texts from Cave Four* (4 fascicles; Washington DC: Biblical Archaeology Society): III.

Weinert, F.D.

1977 'A Note on 4Q159 and a New Theory of Essene Origins', *RevQ* 9: 223-30.

White, S.A.

1987 'A Comparison of the "A" and "B" Manuscripts of the Damascus Document', *RevQ* 48: 537-53.

Winter, P.

1956 'Sadoqite Fragments IV 20, 21 and the Exegesis of Genesis 1:27 in Late Judaism', *ZAW* 68: 71-84.

Wise, M.O.

1990a *A Critical Study of the Temple Scroll from Qumran Cave 11* (Studies in Ancient Oriental Civilization, 49; Chicago: The Oriental Institute of the University of Chicago).

1990b 'The Teacher of Righteousness and the High Priest of the Intersacerdotium: Two Approaches', *RevQ* 14: 587-613.

Wise, M., M. Abegg Jr., and E. Cook
    1996   *The Dead Sea Scrolls: A New Translation* (London: HarperCollins).
van der Woude, A.S.
    1992   'Fünfzehn Jahre Qumranforschung (1974-1988)', *TRu* 57: 1-57.
    1998   'Fifty Years of Qumran Research', in Flint and VanderKam 1998: I, 1-45.
Yadin, Y.
    1983   *The Temple Scroll* (3 vols; Jerusalem: Israel Exploration Society).
Zeitlin, S.
    1952   *The Zadokite Fragments: Facsimile of the Manuscripts in the Cairo Genizah Collection in the Possession of the University Library, Cambridge, England* (JQRMS, 1; Philadelphia: Dropsie College).

Electronic resources

Pinnick, A.   Weekly up-dated on-line bibliography of the Dead Sea Scrolls from 1995 to the present, *The Orion Center for the Study of the Dead Sea Scrolls and Associated Literature Website*: http://orion.mscc.huji.ac.il

Cambridge University Library   Website of the Cambridge University Library Taylor-Schechter Collection: http://www.lib.cam.ac.uk/Taylor-Schechter

INDEXES

INDEX OF REFERENCES

OLD TESTAMENT

QUMRAN INCLUDING JUBILEES

INDEX OF AUTHORS